Law on the Internet: A Practical Guide

First Edition

by

Penelope Lawrence

Solicitor and Attorney at Law (N.Y.)

London · Sweet & Maxwell · 2000

Published in 2000 by
Sweet & Maxwell Limited of
100 Avenue Road, Swiss Cottage, London, NW3 3PF
http://www.sweetandmaxwell.co.uk
Computerset by
Tradespools Ltd.,
Frome, Somerset
Printed in England by Clays Ltd., St Ives plc

A CIP Catalogue record
for this book is available
from the British Library

ISBN 0-421-737-808

FOR DAVID

ACKNOWLEDGMENTS

Sweet & Maxwell would like to thank the following companies, associations and institutions for permission to reproduce screenshots from their websites.

British and Irish Legal Information Institute or BAILII (www.bailii.org)

Coleman Tilley Tarrant Sutton (www.ctts.co.uk)

Epoch Software Holdings Plc (www.DesktopLawyer.net)

Fidler & Pepper Solicitors (www.fidler.co.uk)

Information for Lawyers Limited (www.Infolaw.co.uk)

Law Society's Gazette (www.lawgazette.co.uk)

LawZone (www.lawzone.co.uk)

Allen & Overy (www.newchange.com)

While every care has been taken to establish and acknowledge copyright, and contact the copyright owners, the publishers tender their apologies for any accidental infringement. They would be pleased to come to a suitable arrangement with the rightful owners in each case.

CONTENTS

INTRODUCTION

The first question that has to be asked when writing a book is why? Why are you doing this? Has someone done this before? Can I add anything new? When writing a book about the Internet the question is twofold. It is now not only why are you writing this but also why is it a book?

The answer to the "why are you writing this at all?" question is simple. I needed a book that was a straightforward reference guide to law on the Internet. I couldn't find one that was sufficiently accessible and readable so I decided to write one.

The second question "why is this published as a book and not on a web site?" is also easy to answer. For certain functions the simplicity of a book is hard to beat. It is completely portable. It can be read in the comfy chair in the corner, standing up on the bus and even in the bath. You can even balance it on your lap while you type onto your screen and it is much easier to read.

That said it needs to be considered who this book is for? The answer is young lawyers interested in finding out about the Internet, though some seasoned professionals who are not as Internet savvy as they might wish may find themselves learning quite a lot. It is not aimed at those lawyers adept at all things computer. Technical language and concepts have been kept deliberately simple.

The book covers diverse issues from how to get online to how a law firm can exploit the Internet for their benefit. The book also gives extensive listings of good sites to visit to find U.K. law, E.U. law, International law, legal news, legal forms and anything else legal you can think of.

If you want to find out how important the Internet is now, and how essential it will become for the legal profession in the future then this is a book you need to read. But it will not be enough to just read this book and put it away. It will not have served its purpose unless it also spurs you into action. Learning more about the Internet should change how you work. Students should become familiar with the technology and be happy conducting the majority of their research online. Young lawyers should be using their firms online legal research providers, reading legal news online and pushing those above them for change, law firms themselves should be thinking about upgrading their web site, providing legal services online and incorporating Internet technology into their practices to better serve their clients. If all or any of the above are a consequence of reading this book then it will have succeeded in its mission.

Part A: Orientation

This section is designed to introduce the reader to the Internet by explaining all the basics that it is good to know before going online. If you are new to the Internet a lot that follows will be essential reading. The more experienced user should still find a lot of useful information from the origins of the Internet to questions of security, viruses and Internet law.

CHAPTER ONE

WHAT IS THE INTERNET?

"Suppose all the information stored on computers everywhere were linked, I thought. Suppose I could program my computer to create a space in which anything could be linked to anything." Tim Berners-Lee, Weaving the Web.

The Internet is a network of computers that communicate with each other through the telephone system. It is truly global. The Internet connects governments, schools, homes, rich countries and poor all into one great big web. From your terminal in your front room you can chat to a family caught in the middle of a war zone or send a message to the Prime Minister of Australia. The Internet allows for the almost immediate exchange of information between anyone with a computer and a telephone line anywhere in the world. It is incredible and we haven't started using it yet.

Where did the Internet come from?

Unfortunately, the British can claim no credit for the origins of the Internet. The Internet began to emerge in the early 1960s in America. The American Department of Defense, worried about the possibility of a nuclear strike destroying essential military intelligence, developed a small network of computers that could access all necessary military intelligence. The theory being that if one of the computers in the network was disabled (by a nuclear strike) the network would continue functioning with the remaining computers so the essential information would not be lost. This simple solution to a rather catastrophic scenario bred the germ that eventually developed into the Internet. The Americans called this network ARPAnet (Advanced Research Projects Agency Network). The concept, of a network of computers, was quickly seized upon by the American military as a whole and by the academic community.

Students at Duke University in North Carolina were some of the first to set up a network to exchange information between themselves. Academics were not far behind. The first academic network which linked Yale University and the City University of New York was up and running by the early 1980s. The American Government began to see the possibilities and started investing Government resources in technological development.

The British were not far behind in establishing JANET (the Joint Academic Network). This was a network linking academics at universities across the U.K.

So far, so good, a bunch of American soldiers are communicating with each other on their network and a bunch of American academics are communicating with each other on theirs. While on the other side of the pond the British academics are chatting away too. All of this would have remained useful but low key and not the revolution it has turned into, if it wasn't for the development of gateways. Gateways enabled one network to talk to another. So, the American academics could swap research with the British and vice versa. From this connection of independent networks to each other the Internet was born.

One other major development needs mentioning, this is the World Wide Web. Developed in 1990 at the European Laboratory for Particle Physics in Switzerland by Tim Berners-Lee quoted above. The World Wide Web research expanded the capabilities of the Internet from an essentially static print-based system to the more exciting world of pictures and video images.

What are the Main Functions of the Internet?

This book describes the Internet for lawyers in great detail. But at this point it is worth noting the four broad functions of the Internet.

E-mail

Everyone has heard of e-mail. It is simply the quickest, easiest and cheapest method of communicating with anyone not in the same room as you. If you don't already have your own e-mail address you need to get one.

E-mail is incredibly easy to use. You type your message in the box, add the address, click and it has gone. You can also attach files, pictures or video clips. For more information see p. 27.

The World Wide Web

The World Wide Web is the largest encyclopaedia in the world and the largest shopping mall and the largest games arcade. It is huge. For a lawyer it has a lot to offer, from subscription services to the major journals, case transcripts, statutes, legal magazines and job opportunities. For more information see Part B (Legal Research Online) and Part C (The Best of the Rest: Other Legal Sites).

Usenet or Newsgroups

The Internet provides a forum for people with similar interests to communicate. If you subscribe to a Newsgroup you can send your views on a topic and receive other members views and opinions. There are, of course, a lot of Newsgroups dedicated to legal issues. For more information see p. 28.

Chat

The Internet enables you to chat in real time to anyone on the Internet anywhere. This can, of course, be a social activity as it is for many thousands of people every day. Alternatively, you could use the facilities offered by the Internet for a business conference, with input from colleagues all over the world. For more information see p. 30.

CHAPTER TWO

WHY LAWYERS NEED THE INTERNET

"Starting with baby boomers, the big idea is getting whatever you want right this second, Now. TV 24 hours a day, sex, drugs, all of that . . . so the web delivers in spades—books now, CDs now, flowers and groceries now, stocks, data, letters anything I want I can get now, all of the time by tapping a button." Kurt Anderson, Turn of the Century.

Why do lawyers need the Internet? Because the Internet has and is changing the way our society works and lawyers are part of that society. The Internet changes expectations. It creates the need for instant access and speed of delivery. Successful Internet businesses take paper bound businesses and free them from themselves. No more paper shuffling for travel agents, insurance brokers or banks. So, wherever you are in the legal tree you need to understand the issues facing lawyers and how the Internet is going to effect how legal services are going to be provided over the next few years.

One reason why the Internet is so successful is because it is quicker, simpler and cheaper to use than traditional methods. Take the example of a simple conveyancing transaction (the principles apply equally to large commercial transactions). I have taken it as given that; the solicitor is found and instructed, properties viewed and a mortgage applied for and granted online. But how will technology actually affect the conveyancing process?

A deal has been struck, a price agreed. A basic survey has been carried out. The local authority search and office copies were downloaded from their respective sites within minutes. The preliminary enquiries were e-mailed to the seller and completed online. The sale package and draft contract are e-mailed to the buyer's solicitor. The two sides communicate online. No waiting for letters to be typed, no waiting for the post.

They are nearly ready for exchange. The buyer transfers the deposit monies directly from her bank account to her solicitor's account using her online banking facilities. Contracts are exchanged by telephone and then signed contracts are e-mailed to the other side.

The pre-completion searches are all carried out online. The transfer is signed. The purchase monies transferred. The new title to the property and the building societies mortgage are all registered online.

It is not only in the property sphere that a lot of the transactions will take place online. Most lawyers will already be aware of the court services online forms. They must be, the court services site has approximately 200,000 hits per week. At the moment interactive forms are completed online and then printed off and sent to the relevant court. In line with the governments plans to have all government services available electronically by 2008 it will be possible in the not too distant future to file court documents online. No doubt, in time, the majority of communications with courts across the country will be electronic. We have already had the first judgments issued over the Internet.

In addition to the property transactions and the future of litigation a lot more firms are going to take the leap into e-commerce and provide legal services online.

Intranets

However, the Internet is not only important in the carrying out of transactions it is also important in providing a service to your employees and thereby creating and developing their loyalty to the firm.

Using the technology of the Internet a firm can develop their own internal Internet for fee earners and staff. This internal Internet is known as an Intranet. It uses all the technology of the Internet but connects a web of computers together within an organization rather than outside in the world. Within this limited network a site can be developed that contains all the information that the organization wants to share with its employees. This Intranet can be used to keep staff informed of the firms policies; important new legal developments can be quickly and easily circulated; billing targets and records can be available to the relevant fee earner and client files can even be held electronically, access limited to the relevant fee earner. On the lighter side social events can be advertised, the menus of local restaurants posted and in-jokes and gossip circulated.

Where a firm is separated over several sites, or even where there are just a lot of employees on the one site, an Intranet can bring every employee together online and create an online community for the firm.

While an Intranet shows how Internet technology can be used to increase staff loyalty by increasing their sense of belonging to the firm, the same principles can be applied to improve client loyalty and commitment to the firm.

Extranets

Businesses want a high quality service from their legal advisors. It is only a matter of time before they are demanding more than just access to the relevant fee earner. Clients will want to see their files online to monitor progress and to assess costs. They will want regular updates on important legal issues and a legal team with a detailed knowledge of the workings of their business. This level of transparency between client and lawyer is possible with the development of the Internet.

In order to provide the type of service you want to provide to your clients you will need an Extranet. An Extranet is a secure connection to an Intranet. A firm would be able to invite clients into the areas of their Intranet that were relevant to their business. They could check out who is available for a meeting and how many billable hours the partner in charge has put into their project. Documents could be sent securely over the Extranet and legal updates relevant to the client could be made available. The extra service provided by this direct electronic link increasing the client's commitment to the firm. The availability of Internet technology will in any event create expectations of more transparency and better service.

As an individual lawyer it also needs to be appreciated what an amazing research tool the Internet has become. It is quick and convenient and will undoubtedly replace all but a few law libraries in time. It also, for the first time, gives small practices access to a full law library at a fraction of the cost enabling them to compete on the same terms as their larger competitors.

It is always assumed that the large commercial firms will make full use of new technology but the smaller firms don't need to worry so much. The Internet is different, if smaller firms don't get on board a lot of them just won't exist in five years time. They will either have been swallowed up by their more technologically astute neighbours or forced out of their core businesses by online legal service providers.

So, it doesn't matter whether you are still studying or 10 years qualified or whether you work for a small or large practice. All lawyers need to understand what is happening now and what is likely to happen over the next few years.

CHAPTER THREE

WHAT CAN THE INTERNET DO FOR YOU?

There are a lot of different ways for a lawyer to use the Internet. The following is a list of some of the more likely, no doubt there are others.

E-mail

The main advantage of e-mail is its speed. You don't have to wait for a letter to be typed but, unlike a telephone call, you still have a written record. If you are sending documents attach them to your e-mail.

Find an Agent

You need a solicitor to act as an agent in a far flung part of the world. Look on the web. You will be able to find solicitor's web sites and local bar association sites, all providing valuable information.

Find a Barrister

Sometimes you will need to find a barrister you haven't used before. The web is a good shop window for all the different chambers and a good place to start research into finding the appropriate barrister for your case.

Find an Expert

You need an expert for an urgent matter. The web provides the quickest, easiest and most comprehensive lists of experts in all fields.

Find a New Job

You have just found out from your online news magazine that your firm has merged. You want to move on. The quickest and easiest way to find out the opportunities available to you is to search for a new job online. You can either wander around *The Gazette* or *The Lawyer's* extensive listings (**http://www.lawgazette.co.uk**) (**http://www. interactive-lawyer.com**) or go to one of the specialist recruitment sites (**http://www.qdgroup.com**).

Improve Office Communication with an Intranet

An Intranet uses Internet technology to create a personal Internet for your firm or chambers. It can be used for circulating any information necessary. Bulky documents can be uploaded onto the Intranet and downloaded by any member of staff that needs a hard copy. Social fixtures, interdepartmental football results, anything that increases communication can be kept on the Intranet. An Intranet can be particularly useful if a firm has several offices in different parts of the country or even all over the world. An Intranet can be an invaluable tool to improve communication and to foster a feeling of belonging among staff.

Instant Access to Courts

This hasn't happened yet, but it will. Sometime in the next few years you will be able to file court forms online and a lot more.

Instant Access to Forms

The majority of government forms can already be accessed online. The court service provides a service where nearly all forms that are completed by the parties can be accessed free on the Internet. The forms are completed online and then printed off and sent to the relevant court (**http://www.courtservice.gov.uk**).

The Legal Aid Board web site (**http://www.legal-aid.gov.uk**) can be accessed and forms completed online before being printed off and sent to the relevant area office.

Keep Ahead of New Developments

Do you want to keep in touch with others in your field? Why not join a Newsgroup. You can post queries to other experts in your field or discuss your field of expertise in detail or you can just listen in and see what everyone else is talking about. See p. 29 for details of legal newsgroups.

Keep One Step Ahead of Your Clients with an Extranet

Your firm has a thriving Intranet. You realise that some of your major clients could really benefit from access to your Intranet, but there are also things on the Intranet which are not suitable for a client to see. So, you create an Extranet. This allows a major client to access the parts of your Intranet that are relevant to them. Your client could collect information from the Extranet or post relevant information onto the Extranet.

Keep Up with the News

Not only are *The Lawyer* and *The Gazette* available free online so are several other online legal news services. Why not have a look at LawZone (**http://www.lawzone.co.uk**) or maybe Inbrief (**http://www.inbrief.co.uk**). Just find what you like and bookmark it. Then you will know who is moving where, what firms are merging and all the big news as it happens.

Legal Research

You need to find section 32 of the Channel Tunnel Rail Link Act 1996. You have two choices. The old slow way or the new quick way. Using the old slow way, you get up from your desk and wander down to the library (if you can, send a trainee) and dig out the relevant volume. That is if you are lucky and the correct volume is not already out or incorrectly filed. When you find it you'll need to photocopy the right page, hoping that the photocopier is working.

Alternatively, while sitting at your desk you click on the icon for your Internet Service Provider, access the Internet, call up your bookmarked sites, find the Stationery Office web site (**http://www.hmso.gov.uk**). You locate the Channel Tunnel Rail Link Act 1996 and print off section 32. The easiest part being it will still be there waiting the next time you need to find it.

Provide Online Services

Some law firms have entered the market by providing services online. Quite a few firms have started providing interactive forms on their web sites often for probate work (**http://www.fidler.co.uk**). There will be more to come. See p. 167 for more details.

Publicity and Marketing

This is the first reason why most law firms and chambers go online. The decision to go online is usually prompted by a few clients ringing and saying "I couldn't find your web site or could you give me your web address?"

CHAPTER FOUR

HOW DO I GET ONLINE?

What Do I Need?

If you are setting up at home you need a computer, a screen, a modem and a telephone line. Even if you are using the facilities in your office it helps if you can understand what the basic requirements are and how each piece of the puzzle fits together.

Computer and Screen

So long as your computer is no more than five years old you should have no problems using it to access the Internet. You will need a computer with as much memory as possible. There are two types of memory: RAM (Random Access Memory) and permanent memory on the hard disk. RAM enables your computer to do all the different tasks it needs to. It is sometimes called "function memory". You need as much RAM as you can afford. RAM is measured in bytes therefore you want as many bytes as possible. You need at least 32 megabytes and would be better off with 64 megabytes or more.

The other type of memory is the permanent memory on the hard disk of your computer. You use this memory to store files, Internet pages, games, etc. This type of memory is again measured in bytes or megabytes. You will need at least 800 megabytes, hopefully a lot more.

You will also need a screen or monitor. As you are going to be spending a lot of time staring at this it is best if you get the largest possible.

Modem

A modem is a device that allows computerised information to be transmitted along telephone wires. The majority of computers now have internal modems so you don't even have to think about them. If a computer you are using does not have an internal modem then you need a desktop modem. The thing to think about with a modem is its speed. You want the fastest modem possible. Speed is measured in bits per second or bps. That is the number of bits of computer information that can be transmitted down a telephone wire per second. You want, if possible, to have a modem that operates at 56,000 bps or faster. If your modem is slow it will take longer to access the Internet and your telephone charges will be higher.

Telephone Line

A modem can be plugged into any telephone line to give you access to the Internet. For organisations and individuals that spend a lot time online it may be worthwhile investigating ISDN (Integrated Services Digital Network) access or other similar high speed connecting services. These are quicker and more expensive. A simple phone line (PSTN) is sufficient for most home use.

That is all the hardware you need. The next essential step is to get connected to the Internet. This will require you to choose an Internet Service Provider.

Internet Service Providers

There are two different types of Internet Service Provider. Firstly, the online service provider. This type of company typically gives access to the Internet and provides its own content. There is usually a monthly fee and telephone call costs (see below on pricing). The best known Online Service Providers are America On Line (AOL) (**http://www.aol.com**) and Compuserve (**http://www.compuserve.com**). The advantages of these providers are their ease of use and generally free support services. To hook up with one of these providers you need to obtain one of their free discs and follow the prompts on screen. You will be asked to provide your credit card details so the monthly fee can be deducted. See p. 207 for contact details.

The true Internet Service Provider is now nearly always free except for telephone charges (but see below on pricing). All you need to do is obtain the disc, insert into your computer and follow the commands on your screen. This will connect you to the Internet. There are several good ones to choose from. The best known are Dixon's Freeserve (**http://www.freeserve.co.uk**), Virgin (**http://www.virgin.net**), Demon (**http://www.demon.net**), WH Smith On-Line (**http://www.whsmith.co.uk**), BT Internet (**http://www.btinternet.com**) and U-Net (**http://www.u-net.net**). See p. 207 for contact details.

Pricing

As you can see from the above the only real issue in the cost of access to the Internet is the cost of telephone calls and this is changing fast. BT's monopoly as the gatekeeper to the Internet has been removed, this should allow for true competition on price and bring the U.K. towards the situation in the States with flat rate pricing irrespective of how long you spend online. In addition to this I would also guess that there will be a myriad of deals linking in with your regular phone usage, cable television usage and peak or off-peak use of the Internet. With this uncertainty and the probability of falling costs it is best not to tie yourself into a long term contact.

What Next?

Once you have chosen your Internet Service Provider, put their disc into your computer and follow the prompts on screen, you will be online. The first thing you will see is a screen with a set of buttons. This screen and the functions it possesses is your browser. You will use your browser to navigate the World Wide Web. To access any of the functions available you need to use your mouse to move the cursor to click on the relevant button. Look at the picture of the screen on the adjacent page and work your way around the screen identifying all the important buttons.

1. **Home**—If this button is chosen your browser will take your screen back to the page you have chosen as your homepage.

2. **Back**—This will take you back to the web page you last visited.

3. **Forward**—This will take you forward from the page you are currently on. This can only be used if you have already used the back button.

4. **Refresh**—This button is used if a web page you are trying to view has failed to load, loaded incorrectly or needs reloading to update. If you press the refresh button the computer will reload.

5. **Stop**—This stops a page from loading. This button can be very useful when a page is taking ages to load and you want to give up and move onto something else.

6. **Read or Mail**—This button will give you access to your e-mail folder. On AOL there is also a write button for writing e-mails.

7. **Help**—This directs you to support services available, often online. Watch out! This can be expensive. Some free service providers use their help desks as a method of boosting revenues.

8. **Favourites or Bookmark**—This button enables you to store your favourite web sites. So, with a couple of clicks you can access your favourite sites again without time consuming searching or having to remember a web address.

9. **Address or Locator**—This shows you the web address of the site you are currently visiting. You also use this space to type in the address of a web site you want to visit, press enter and you will be taken to the new site.

10. **Status bar**—The status bar shows you the web address of a link your cursor is pointing at.

11. **Scroll bar**—Use cursor to scroll up and down.

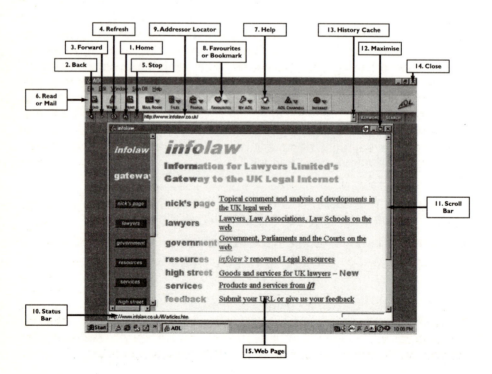

12. **Maximise**—Use this button to increase or decrease size of window.

13. **History Cache**—Select this button to see a list of recently visited sites. Link directly to a site by clicking on a name in the list.

14. **Close**—Choose to close screen.

15. **Web Page**—The actual page from the web site that you can see on your browser.

Surfing the Web

One of the first things you will want to do once you are online is to practice surfing the web. In order to do this you will need to employ a search engine.

Search Engines

However you have chosen to access the Internet you need to understand search engines. A search engine is a computer program that trawls around the Internet to help you find what you are looking for. The search engine will scurry around the Internet and come back to you with a list of objects that match your search (a "hit"). These will normally be presented to you in some kind of logical order, starting off with the closest match to your search, proceeding downwards to the completely irrelevant. If your search is very general don't be surprised if the search engine comes back with a very large number of hits. Sometimes your screen will say there were 1,700,364 pages that matched your search criteria and start off by showing you the first 10. If this is the case you need to narrow down your search and improve your search techniques.

So, how do you choose a search engine? If you subscribe to an online service provider your primary search engine will have been chosen for you. This does not mean you have to stick with this one. If you are not happy with your search results you can access another search engine by typing their web address into your address box and pressing enter on the keyboard. You will now be able to use this search engine. If you are using an Internet Service Provider you will usually have to choose a search engine to do your trawling through the web for you. It is probably best to try out as many search engines as you can and then stick with the one that gives you the best results.

21

This is because each search engine has a slightly different method of searching and different combinations of words will come up with different results.

The following are some of the best search engines (but there are many others):

http://www.altavista.co.uk

http://alltheweb.com

http://www.google.com

http://www.lawrunner.com

http://web.lawcrawler.com/countries/uk.html

http://www.dogpile.com

For general search engines, out of the above list, altavista is probably my favourite, although maybe as much from familiarity as for any other reason. Google.com is a newcomer and uses a different system. Google ranks pages according to their popularity assessing this by the number of links to the page. In a brief test run it appeared to be very effective. Another newcomer, and from my experience a very fast and effective one, is alltheweb.com. Lawcrawler and Lawrunner are search engines programmed specifically to search for law materials. Both focus on law sites eradicating the majority of the irrelevant material. They are U.S. based engines but it is possible to focus on searching U.K. legal sites. Dogpile on the other hand takes a different approach by searching the other search engines.

All of the above sites give advice on how to achieve the best search results. It is worth spending the time reading the search tips of the search engine you choose to use. Good searching techniques can save you a lot of grief. Some simple rules that apply to nearly all search engines are:

1. Make your search as specific as possible. Use several words to narrow down your search, *i.e.* expert witness forensic psychology. This search will throw up pages with any of these words in. If you only want pages that contain all these words use the " + " symbol as explained below.

2. If you are looking for an exact phrase put quotation marks around it. The search engine will only look for those words when they appear together as a phrase, *i.e.* "Lord Mackay of Clashfern".

3. Use lower case text in your searches. This will give you lowercase and uppercase results. If you search using uppercase you will only get uppercase results.

4. You can include or exclude words by using the symbols "+" and "−". To include a word place a "+" sign before the word. To exclude a word put a "−" sign before the word, *i.e.* injunctions + doctors − matrimonial.

5. By typing an "*" at the end of a word you can search for different forms of the same word, *i.e.* conveyanc*. This would search for conveyances, conveyancing and conveyancer. You would probably end up with a lot of sites for various types of transport so I would also add "− automobiles" and "− cars"!

The only way to become an expert using the Internet is to spend five minutes practicing. Below is an example of a search for a computer expert. Why not see how long it takes you to come up with a choice of five forensic psychologists?

You have an unusual problem. Your client was dismissed from his senior position at a well-known bank. He has been accused of sending abusive e-mails to his colleagues. Your client does not dispute that the e-mails appear to have originated from his machine but he denies that he sent them. He is suing for wrongful dismissal. You need an expert and quick. You have never used an expert in this area before so you haven't got one on file. Where do you look? The easiest way would be to go to a legal portal (**http://www.uklegal.com**) or news magazine (**http://www.lawzone.co.uk**) and link to their list of experts. Alternatively, you may have bookmarked a good register of experts last time you were searching for one (**http://www.academy-experts.org**).

It took less than five minutes to find a choice of experts in this field. The majority of experts listed maintained their own Internet presence so it was possible to link directly to their web sites and check out their experience, availability and other details.

Searching a Website

Once you have found the web site you are looking for, the searching is not over yet. A lot of web sites are enormous, the volume of information on some sites would fill a library. It is therefore going to be necessary to be able to search the sites themselves. Sites with a lot of information stored on them all have site specific search engines. The principles for searching these sites are basically the same except that you will often see on site the term "Boolean operators". This means that the search engine will understand a particular coded way of writing. The most common Boolean operators are the words "and", "or", "near" and "not". Using one of these words in your search will have specific effects. For instance if you search for cats *and* dogs then the search engine will look for results with both these terms. Alternatively, and usually more effectively, if you use "near" in your searches the search engine will look for your search terms within ten words of each other. So, if you were searching for: internet *near* privacy *near* law hopefully you would find information on privacy law on the Internet and not a lot of information on the Internet and a lot of information on privacy, etc. The Boolean operator "not" operates in a similar way by excluding certain categories from your search.

A lot of sites provide information on how to use their search engine. On a site that you are going to be spending a lot of time on it is worth printing off the search information, reading it and keeping it to hand for the more advanced search techniques.

CHAPTER FIVE

COMMUNICATING ON THE WEB

E-mail

E-mail stands for electronic mail. The majority of Internet Service Providers come with e-mail software. If you do not have e-mail facilities already you can download stand alone e-mail software. Two of the most popular and free applications would be: Netscape at **http://www.netscape.com** or Outlook at **http://www.microsoft.com**.

Once you have e-mail software installed it could not be easier. Open e-mail by clicking on an envelope icon or a button that says e-mail. Then type in an e-mail address and your message and click send. The e-mail is sent over the phone lines that connect your computer to the Internet and on to the e-mail address that you specified.

This section is going to look first at how to use e-mail and issues like offline e-mailing and finding e-mail addresses. Then at the end of the section I am going to look at a few of the issues connected with e-mail that are particularly relevant to law firms.

Offline E-Mailing

A good tip is to always prepare or read e-mails offline. There is no need for you to be connected to the Internet to write e-mails. Turn on your computer and click on the icon for your Internet service. Before you connect to the Internet you can press your mail or write button and prepare all your e-mails. Don't forget to save them to send later. Similarly, when you are connected to the Internet you can save any received e-mails and read them offline also.

E-Mail Addresses

An e-mail address is made up of a simple code. Starting at the beginning:

- The first letters in an e-mail address signify the name of the sender. So, taking an example, an e-mail address could start with kjones standing for Karen Jones. Note that e-mail addresses are usually all lowercase. Incorrectly typed cases can lead to misdirected e-mail. It is often the case that your own name is not available. In this situation you will need to be imaginative.

- The next part of an e-mail address is the "@" or "at" sign.

- After this comes the name of the computer where your mailbox is. This could be "demon" or "freeserve" or "aol" or countless others.

- The next piece of the code signifies whether the computer your mailbox is in is a business or government site, etc. The code **.co** signifies a business site as does **.com**. While **.ac** or **.edu** means a university or other educational establishment and **.gov** means a government site and **.org** means a site for any kind of organisation.

- The last piece of the puzzle signifies where the address is in the world. The code **.uk** shows the address to be British and **.ie** to be Irish. The most well known of all **.com** as well as signifying a business address also shows it to be an American address or one with an American Internet Service Provider. It is a simple process of deduction to work out the country of origin of most e-mail addresses.

Finding E-Mail Addresses

There are an awful lot of e-mail addresses in the world. Finding an e-mail address off the Internet can be like looking for the proverbial needle in a haystack, but worse. It is easier to find the address of a business or organisation rather than an individual. Sometimes it is just easier to try guessing or telephoning for it!

If you do want to try to find an e-mail address there are several directories on the Internet you can try. One of the most straightforward to use for U.K. addresses is the yellow pages web directory. This can be found at **http://www.yell.co.uk.** or try **http://www.scoot.com**.

Address Book

Once you have found the e-mail address you have been looking for make sure you save it in your address book. Nearly all e-mail programs have an address book capability, if yours doesn't, change your program. It is too useful to do without. Whenever you receive an e-mail check out whether you want to keep the address. If you do just open your address book and choose the relevant options. Then whenever you want to e-mail the same person again it is simple to transfer the address directly from your address book to your e-mail screen.

Attachments

E-mails are usually short and to the point. Sometimes you will want to send a long document, graphics or a video clip over the Internet. This is done by attaching the files that contain these to an e-mail.

The easiest way to attach a file to your e-mail is to use the attach button. This often looks like a paper clip and is situated on your e-mail window. Just click the attach button, type in the name and location of the file you want to send and attach this file to your e-mail. Alternatively, you could choose attach file from a drop down menu.

There are a couple of warnings along the way. Don't send large files, unless you have warned the recipient and they have agreed. Files can take a long time to download. Also make sure that the file, when it arrives, will be in a format their computer can read. There is nothing more frustrating than spending ages downloading a file you didn't ask for and then discovering it looks as if it was written in Aramaic. This happens because files sent over the Internet are often compressed or zipped. Essentially they are squashed up to make it quicker and easier to send them. What you need to be able to do is to unzip them.

To unzip files it is well worth investing in a simple piece of software. You can buy the ZipMagic or Winzip discs and load onto your computer or download from the Internet from **http://www.winzip.com** or **http://www.zipmagic.com**.

It is also possible to send pictures or video clips as attachments. These can be very large files and often need specific software to download again check with the recipient before you send.

E-Mail Issues

Some e-mail issues are of particular interest to lawyers. I am going to briefly look at three of these: permanency, e-mail policies in the workplace and privilege waivers in e-mails.

Permanency

It is easy to forget, because e-mail is so easy to send that it is not equivalent to a phone call. It does not disappear when it has been read and deleted. It will leave a trail and solicitors advising clients should make sure that they are aware of this. A client may send an inappropriate internal e-mail not thinking that it could be subject to discovery. If people were aware of how truly permanent e-mails are, they would probably say a lot less in them.

E-Mail Policies

It is becoming more common for firms to think about introducing e-mail policies. Are employees allowed to use e-mail facilities for their personal use? If they are what amounts to a reasonable use? Could the firm be liable if an employee harasses female members of staff by e-mail? Should the firm be monitoring employees use of e-mail to ensure that it is not being used for illegal or damaging purposes? All of these issues and others need to be addressed and a decision made whether to bring in a formal e-mail policy.

Privilege Waivers in E-Mail?

Lawyers also need to think about whether to include privilege waivers as standard in their e-mails. Richard Hodgson at Design Chambers includes the following in all e-mails: "This e-mail (including any attachments) is private and confidential, may attract legal privilege, and is only intended for the named recipient(s)."

Newsgroups and Mailing Lists

Newsgroups and mailing lists are methods of using the Internet to exchange information and ideas on a specific topic with people anywhere in the world. There are quite subtle differences between the two forms of communication, so I will deal with them separately.

Mailing Lists

If you subscribe to a mailing list, for instance, on U.K. planning law, you would receive in your mailbox the thoughts, opinions and ideas of the other subscribers. You would also be able to e-mail off your own opinions. The standard of debate can be very high or abysmally low. It all depends on the mailing list you subscribe to. As a general rule the standard of debate in a private mailing list, *i.e.* one that only permits certain people access will be immeasurably higher. A lot of academic mailing lists are run on these lines.

A lot of the better ones you will find out about are through word of mouth. Alternatively, a list of mailing lists can be found at Liszt.com (**http://www.liszt.com**) or check out the U.S. legal portals (**http://findlaw.com**) and follow the links for mailing lists or newsgroups. This is a good way to find legal mailing lists. Once you have searched and found your mailing list you will need to subscribe, this is done by sending an e-mail to the mailing list. Beware: you might be turned down!

Newsgroups

Newsgroups are a bit different. First, they are maintained by your Internet Service Provider and, therefore, they are not as private and there can be an element of censorship involved. Like mailing lists there are newsgroups available on every topic under the sun including quite a few devoted to law. Access to newsgroups is public so the level of legal debate can often leave something to be desired. Newsgroup discussions are arranged in threads to help you follow one particular discussion rather than be distracted by comments off topic.

The easiest way to find newsgroups is through your Internet Service Provider. There will usually be a newsgroup button or you will find newsgroups on your dropdown menu in your e-mail application. Once you have accessed newsgroups, search to find the newsgroup that matches your interests. Alternatively, you can go to Liszt.com (**http://www.liszt.com**), this site has an extensive listing of newsgroups. When you have found your newsgroup you will need to subscribe. This is very straightforward and enables you to join in the discussion as opposed to just reading other people's views. It is usually advised that you lurk around a site you like the look of, read the messages and to follow a debate before you jump in. That way you won't make a fool of yourself by jumping in off topic.

Chat

It is also possible to take part in "live" chat online. This is not going to be of much use to most lawyers except as a way of passing a rare idle moment. Chat is conducted in a format called Internet Relay Chat or IRC. IRC is split up into hundreds of chat rooms or channels each discussing a different topic. You can access chat rooms directly through your Internet Service Provider or in simpler terms this means when you log onto the Internet you will see a button to choose chat. This will take you through to the chat rooms where you search for a topic that interests you. You usually need specific software to take part in the chat. If this isn't part of the package already on your computer it is simple to download a good program, try going to **http:// www.liszt.com**, choose chat and you will be offered the option to download software.

One way that lawyers could use chat technology to their benefit would be by setting up a real time Internet conference-chat connecting terminals all over the world. This can be done simply and securely with only a little technical knowledge.

Netspeak

If you communicate on the Internet you will probably have come across netspeak. Some users of the Internet have developed a system of abbreviations that are quite commonly used. I have particularly found this to be the case with the Internet savvy Americans. The British tend to be a bit more reserved about this type of thing. It is probably the terrible fear that they will make a gaff and get it horribly wrong. Anyway, if you receive e-mail, subscribe to a mailing list, frequent chat rooms or belong to a newsgroup you need to be aware what the others are talking about. Here is a list of some of the most common abbreviations:

ASAP as soon as possible
AWK   away from keyboard
B4   before
BRB   be right back
CUL   see you later
FOC   free of charge
FYA   for your amusement
FYIO for your eyes only
FYI   for your information
IME   in my experience

IMHO in my humble opinion
IOW   in other words
KISS   keep it simple stupid
NRN   no reply necessary
OBTW oh by the way
OTT   over the top
ROFL rolls on the floor laughing
RSN   real soon now
RUOK are you OK?
TIA   thank you in advance
TTFN ta ta for now
TVM   thank you very much

You also need to watch out for what are known as smileys. These are little pictures made with symbols on the keyboard. They are usually written to denote some kind of emotion. Like abbreviations there are a lot of them. Here are some of the more commonly used:

:-)   smiling
:-(sad
:-O   shouting
:'-(crying
:-S   oops!

Netiquette

As well as being aware of net speak it is also important to understand netiquette. Netiquette is made up of some very basic rules of behaviour for web users. The most well known are:

- Don't spam. This means do not send junk mail to mailboxes or to newsgroups. It makes people very cross and can get you thrown off your Internet Service Provider if they catch you.

- Read the FAQs before asking a question. These frequently asked questions will be found on a lot of sites and newsgroups. You just look daft if you ask a question that is in the FAQs.

- Don't write in capitals. It is considered to be shouting.

- Never send chain mails.

- Don't post adverts on newsgroups.

- Don't post get rich quick schemes on newsgroups.

CHAPTER SIX

FREQUENTLY ASKED QUESTIONS

Security

Security is the most common reason cited to me by lawyers when explaining their reluctance to become involved in the provision of legal services using new technology. It is undoubtedly a valid concern and without the proper measures a law firm could be opening themselves up to a negligence claim if an unfortunate e-mail fell into the wrong hands or a determined hacker downloaded a clients' file. But it also has to be realised that the majority of security lapses do not come from the outside. It is far more likely that a security leak will come from the inside, bearing this in mind it is very important that security includes looking at the access employees have to the network as well as the far more remote threat of the unknown.

Confidentiality of information can be protected in lots of different ways. One way would be to provide access to certain types of information only to those who needed it. This type of security is called access control. The most frequently used type of access control is the use of passwords for access to restricted areas. The biggest problem with this is human failing. People forget things, especially things like passwords so they write the password on a post-it and stick it to the monitor or somewhere equally daft. If a password system is in use it is important that all employees are educated about the need to maintain secrecy. A further aspect of controlling access is allowing access to different people on different bases. The lead lawyer on a transaction would be given access to all the documents in a virtual dealroom on a read and write basis, while the trainee could have read only access unless specifically authorised.

It is important to remember that the security of a firm's information technology database is not just concerned with the issue of confidentiality although this is often uppermost in a lawyer's mind. The issue of integrity of data also has to be considered. Integrity of data ensures that data cannot be modified either accidentally or unintentionally. Where the accuracy of information held is crucial, like in a lawyer's office, it is important to use the correct processes to ensure that integrity is maintained. One way of doing this would be to protect sensitive data by using encryption to prevent unauthorised individuals from making use of the data should they get their hands on it.

A further aspect of security, the availability of information, also, has to be considered. It could be very damaging to a firm if important data was deleted from their files or made inaccessible. To assist in preventing this it is helpful if access to the network from outside is controlled. To do this a firewall is used. A firewall is a set of computer programs, often in a separate computer, located at the gateway to a network. Its purpose is to control the types of data that can flow between the public (Internet) and the private network. The existence of a firewall can prevent intrusions from unwanted parties attempting to interfere with the availability of data. Another aspect of availability of data is the existence of a secure back-up system. This involves not only back-up should the computer network fail or be compromised but also back-up for power supplies.

E-Mail

For lawyers the primary issue involved is the security of confidential e-mails. It is essential to ensure that no person can intercept or read e-mail en route from or to a lawyer's offices. It is often presumed that e-mail travels directly from A to B. This is not how the Internet works. E-Mail doesn't travel directly from the sender to the recipient. It makes stops along the way at gateways to different networks. It is more than feasible that e-mails could be intercepted at this point. It is probably no more risky than someone intercepting your mail but it is a real risk and steps need to be taken to reduce it. The solution to this type of security problem is to invest in secure e-mail services that encrypt or codify e-mail. If a sound encryption system is in place sending and receiving e-mails is as secure as sending a letter by post.

Viruses

Computer viruses do exist but not nearly as many as the scare stories would have you believe. For every real virus there are a thousand myths. If a few basic rules are followed viruses should not pose a great threat to a legal practice. The rules should be well publicised across the practice and adhered to strictly. The first and most important rule is to ensure that the firm invests in good anti-virus software and that this software is regularly updated. Secondly, employees must be forbidden from loading onto their work computers floppy discs that have not originated with the firm or that have been taken home and used on home computers and then brought back to work. The third rule is to warn employees not to open or download attachments to e-mails if they are not sure of the provenance of the e-mail. If these simple rules are kept viruses should not be a problem. But as a final rule, if the worst does happen and all the files of your firm are wiped out in one terrible minute, make sure that adequate back-up systems are already in place to rescue the situation.

What Law Governs the Internet?

While the Internet itself is new, the majority of legal challenges it raises are not. There is relatively little "Internet Law" as such. The rules of contract, defamation, copyright and trademarks have been adapted to fit the Internet. In most cases coping perfectly adequately with the new situation. Defamation law was used in the *Godfrey* v. *Demon Internet Ltd* [1998] Q.B.D. (**http://www.courtservice.gov.uk**) case to establish the liability of an Internet Service Provider for defamation, domain name pirates have been prevented from stealing companies names and images by copyright and trademark law. The law has generally proved to be remarkably flexible but this said some areas have emerged as requiring legislative support. In these key areas the government and the European Union have stepped in with four new proposals:

- Electronic Commerce Directive

- Electronic Communications Bill

- Electronic Signatures Directive

- The Brussels Regulation

It should be noted that at the time of writing all these proposals are in the draft or consultation stage and, unfortunately, no dates for implementation have been given. A brief explanation of the main issues raised by the above proposals follows:

Electronic Commerce Directive

The original draft of the Electronic Commerce Directive can be found at **http://www.ispo.cec.be/ecommerce/docs/legalen.pdf** and commentary by the Department of Trade and Industry with a lot of useful links can be found at **http://www.dti.gov.uk/cii/ecomdirective/index.htm.**

The aim of the draft Electronic Commerce Directive is to remove the obstacles to the free flow of online services in Europe posed by divergent national legislation and jurisprudence. It aims to do this by tackling five key issues, these are:

1. Defining the place of establishment of Information Society Service Providers (Internet Service Providers).

2. Defining a commercial communication (advertising, marketing, etc.) and imposing rules of clarity and transparency on these marketing activities over the Internet. In particular, for professionals like lawyers a general principle is laid down that commercial communications are permitted, but that they must respect the rules of professional ethics in the codes of conduct of their professional association. The current situation is that if a lawyer's web site is aimed at a country other than England and Wales, it must comply with any restrictions imposed by that countries professional association as well as their country of origin. The proposals in the directive would make it easier for lawyers to market their services in Europe as they would only have to comply with the codes of conduct from their country of origin.

3. Simplifying the online conclusion of contracts. National States will need to adjust their national legislation to remove restrictions on the formation of contracts that do not facilitate the making of contracts online. The proposal also adopts the country of origin principle, though a number of derogations have been allowed. Thus, a provider of online services would only need to comply with the regulations in their country of origin and not in all 15 member states. This eases the regulatory burden on providers but leads consumer groups to fear that service providers will flock to the E.U. country with the least protection for consumers.

4. Clarifying the responsibility of online service providers for the transmitting and storing of third party information. The proposal establishes a "mere conduit" exemption and limits service providers liabilities for other "intermediary activities".

5. Strengthening of existing enforcement mechanisms, promoting the development of codes of conduct at national level and facilitating the setting up of effective cross-border alternative dispute resolution systems.

Electronic Communications Bill and E.U. Electronic Signatures Directive

The Electronic Communications Bill (**http://www.publications .parliament.uk**) is consistent with and seeks to implement certain provisions of the Electronic Signatures Directive (1999/93/EC) which was itself intended to harmonise the legal acceptance of electronic signatures throughout the E.U. The Electronic Communications Bill aims to help build confidence in electronic commerce by:

- providing for an approvals scheme for businesses providing cryptography services such as the provision of electronic signatures and confidentiality services like encryption;
- the legal recognition of electronic signatures; and
- the removal of other legislative obstacles to the use of electronic communication and storage of data.

The Brussels Regulation

The European Commission has published a proposal for a new regulation to deal with the problem of jurisdiction of contracts in the E.U. This has particular relevance to those interested in the jurisdiction of contracts entered into on the Internet. The regulation proposes to bring into the body of European Law an updated version of the 1968 Brussels Convention on Jurisdiction and the Enforcement of Judgements in Civil and Commercial Matters. The Brussels Regulation would ensure on the one hand that a consumer could sue, on a consumer contract, either in their country of their domicile or in the country of origin of the supplier of the service. The supplier of the service, on the other hand would be limited to bringing proceedings only in the consumer's country of domicile. This provision is limited to consumer contracts that are concluded with a supplier whose activities are pursued in the consumer's country or directed towards that consumer's country. The difficult question will be in deciding in the case of Internet companies whether their services are directed at a particular country?

Although the government and the E.U. have a stated aim of minimal regulatory intervention in the Internet this aim is probably not enough to stop the development of a new legal specialty of Internet law. Governments find it very hard to leave well alone. The first tough case will almost certainly see them rushing in with more regulations creating, of course, lots more work for lawyers.

Can You Rely on Law on the Web?

In the next section of the book there are a large number of web sites containing a lot of law, but can a law student or lawyer rely on law obtained from the Internet? I would argue that the Internet is not really the point in this debate. It is just a method of delivery. If you think of web pages like books written by different authors, then the same decisions on values to be attached apply. In the real world, decisions are made daily by law students and practitioners on the standing of various legal resources, the same basic rules apply on the Internet. A statute published by the Stationery Office would be as reliable on the Internet as in a paper form while an unrefereed article in an unknown publication shouldn't be relied upon wherever you find it.

That is not to say that there are not problems. First, the general unfamiliarity with the Internet of legal professionals leads to understandable reluctance to rely on electronic information when, for so long, paper and ink were gospel. In many ways a far more serious problem is that of citation. There have been established practices in publishing for a long time giving uniform citation in cases and statutes. There is not, as yet, such an agreement among Internet publishers and there are technical difficulties in ensuring that any citation system adopted is interpreted identically by the myriad computers and browsers that will need to adopt it.

Given the unfamiliarity of the surroundings, how should you evaluate a web site? I would suggest applying a few basic rules:

• Check who publishes the site and/or who wrote the content

As a general rule the information on the sites of well respected legal publishers, governments and respected companies tend to come with a guarantee of authenticity. Governments and corporations have reputations to lose. It is important to them and to us that their sites are accurate. A lot of university sites especially in the States are also of a very high quality, but check whether the site is the work of students or faculty?

- Check the information on the site

One of the essentials of any good web site is a last updated tag. It is important for you to know that the law is current. If the tag is way out of date: beware. Maybe the authors aren't so careful about the content either? It is equally worrying if there is no update tag, how are you supposed to know if it was yesterday or last year that the site was updated?

Also, check the mission statement of the site (if there is one). Is the publishers purpose to promulgate particular views?

- Are the publishers objective?

Look around the site, is there any advertising? Who is it by? Is it likely to lead to conflict of interest with the content of the site? If so, take care.

Keep up to date with legal sources on the Internet. Be aware of recommended sites and equally be aware of sites that have been criticized for inaccuracies.

- Verify

Don't rely purely on one source for all your legal information. Check the facts. Don't presume that because you linked from a well known source that the web page you arrive at is equally reliable. That is not how the Internet works!

Be particularly careful if you are surfing outside your jurisdiction. Pre-Internet it was very difficult to research the law of a foreign jurisdiction, now it is simple. But, we have less knowledge of who to trust outside our own country. There are not that many people who could name the major legal publishers in Australia, Ireland or Iceland and therefore a lot more care must be taken in establishing the reliability of your sources when surfing overseas.

Are You Ready for the Web?

Having read all the first part of this book if you can answer the following questions you are on your way:

- Do you know the difference between a search engine and a web browser?
- Can you name your Internet Service Provider?
- Does spam only come in a tin?
- Do you know what a newsgroup is and how to join one?
- Can you explain what a modem does?
- What are viruses?
- How will the Electronic Commerce Directive change the law?

Part B: Legal Research Online

CHAPTER ONE

FINDING LAW ONLINE

This section sets out where to find law for free on the Internet. As there is so much available this can only be an introduction but I have tried to include those sites that I think are really worth visiting.

All efforts have been made to ensure that URLs given are accurate but with the speed of change a few will be out of date. Hopefully there is sufficient information in the book as a whole to enable you to find an alternative route to a particular site.

Domestic Law

Legislation

Legislation lends itself to being transported onto a media like the Internet. It is therefore surprising to find that at present it is poorly catered for. Hopefully this is about to change with the arrival of the statute law database. Once this is up and running and with any luck free; lawyers and law students will have valuable access to statute law online.

Primary legislation

HMSO

At the moment the main site for U.K. statutes is Her Majesty's Stationery Office Site (**http://www.hmso.gov.uk**). The full text of Acts of Parliament dating from January 1996 are available on site. A few other earlier Acts are also printed in full. These are the Data Protection Act 1984, the Criminal Appeal Act 1995 and the Disability Discrimination Act 1995.

The major problem with the publication of Acts on the HMSO site is the fact that it is very difficult to tell whether any particular section of an Act is in force or has been repealed. The Act is published on the Internet exactly as it was passed by Parliament. Her Majesty's Stationery Office inform me that they are under a statutory duty to publish the Act in this way. For this reason the Acts on site are only of practical use if you also have updating facilities for the Acts. The solution to this problem is the statute law database due to go online in late 2000.

Use this site for:

- Researching the original text of recent Acts.

Statute Law Database

The statute law database is a project of the Statutory Publication Office of the Lord Chancellor's Department. The database will house a complete set of Acts of Parliament from the Magna Carta to the present day. It will be possible to establish the law as it stands today and also to undertake a historical search to establish the law as it stood on any day from February 1, 1991. The Acts will be updated with amendments, commencement orders and repeals as they happen. The search facilities will be by title, date and natural language and Boolean operators.

The department had not decided at the time of writing how, to whom or in what format the service is going to be made available. Or alternatively the decision whether to make the service freely available to the public had yet to be taken, no doubt the treasury is pressuring for a return on their years of investment. In order to keep up to date with the situation check in at the Lord Chancellor's Department web site (**http://www.open.gov.uk/lcd/**).

When it arrives use this site for:

- All statutory research.
- Updating knowledge in areas of statutory law.

The British and Irish Legal Information Institute

The Bailii Project (**http://www.bailii.org**) intends to provide comprehensive and free access to case and statute law on the Internet for the five jurisdictions that make up the British Isles. The idea behind the project comes from Australia where the Australasian Legal Information Institute (AustLII) provides an Internet service where all statutes and case law are published free with full hyperlinking between resources and an excellent search engine.

Lords Saville and Brooke set the ball rolling when sitting in judgment together in the Chancery Division case of *Bannister* v. *SGB plc and Others* (1997). They urged that the judgment be immediately published on the Internet raising awareness of the issue and setting a precedent. The Bailii project aims to build a site similar to the Australian site here. The project is quite advanced and a pilot site is already up and running. Unfortunately, there was no U.K. legislation on the site at the time of writing but it would seem obvious that when the statute law database comes online that access is to be provided through the Bailii site.

When statute law comes online use this site for:

- Statutory research.

- General legal research in all areas of law.

- Legal research for Scottish, Welsh, Northern Irish and Irish Law.

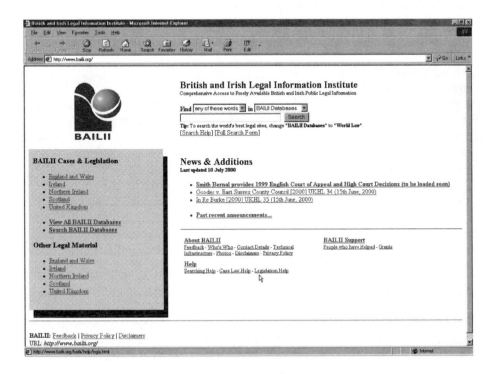

Secondary Legislation

HMSO

The main source for statutory instruments on the Internet is the HMSO site (**http://www.hmso.gov.uk**). All statutory instruments published from 1997 up to the present date are available in full text. Draft statutory instruments are also available. It is possible to search by number and year as well as using the search engine on site using either a natural language search or Boolean operators.

The statutory instrument site can be used to check whether sections of recent Acts have come into force.

Enter the name of the Act you want to search against and the words "commencement orders" and among other information brought up onto the screen will be a list of commencement orders relating to that Act.

Use this site for:

- Researching recent statutory instruments.
- Finding recent commencement orders.

House of Commons

On the House of Commons site (**http://www.parliament.uk**) follow the links to "publications on the Internet" and then to "statutory instruments".

Use this site for:

- Following the progress of a statutory instrument through the House of Commons.

Subscription Services

There are no subscription services at present purely for statute law. Subscription services that contain statute law and other sources are dealt with under subscription services, see p. 111.

Case Law

All lawyers and law students need to have access to a database of case law. So, in this section I have set out a lot of sites offering free access to case law. But, as no free service is sufficiently comprehensive, I have also included reviews of the major case law subscription providers. See also the section on legal research on the Internet on p. 111 for details of subscription sites with a selection of different databases including case law.

The best site for free access to case law has to be the House of Lords, it delivers more law and delivers it quickly and at the moment the deficiencies in the search facilities do not have too great an impact. I would also bookmark the Daily Law Notes service from The Incorporated Council of Law Reporting. The Court Service site on the other hand at the time of writing was a nightmare, with very, very slow connection times. Of the subscription services there is really not much between them. Choosing between the two I would choose New Law but that is probably as much because I am more familiar with this service than any great difference between the two.

House of Lords

In terms of courts the House of Lords is leading the way in its response to the challenges of the Internet. To access the House of Lords judgments go to the parliament site (**http://www. parliament.uk**), choose: (1) House of Lords; (2) judicial work and judgments; and (3) judgments. Following these links will bring you to a list of judgments.

All judgments delivered since November 14, 1996 are online. New judgments are online within two hours of delivery. Judgments are listed by date and alphabetical order.

There is a search facility available but I found it next to impossible to use. I might have tried on a bad day and will return for a further try. At the moment the inadequacies of the search facility are not that serious as there are relatively few cases. The actual search options available can also appear a bit confusing. The speaker and question number boxes are not relevant as these are for searches of Hansard. So, if you are searching for a case, leave these boxes blank. Search facilities on site at the moment are due for updating, so hopefully it will have substantially improved soon.

One of the major problems with case reports on the Internet, which is illustrated by the House of Lords site and the Court Service site, is the lack of page and paragraph numbering. How is anyone to know what exact part of the case you are referring to if you have taken the Internet as your source. There are two reasons for this, the first is technical. When a page is displayed on your computer your browser has interpreted the information provided in a particular way. Different browsers will set the information out in different ways on different computers. The second reason is that there is not, as yet, an agreed standard for Internet citations. In the not too distant future both problems should hopefully be solved.

One improvement that could be made to the House of Lords site would be the inclusion of hyperlinks to other sites or cases. Hopefully, as this and other sites develop and databases are expanded, an effective search facility will be developed and hyperlinks will be added to automatically link you to cases considered in judgment, cases reversed, cases considered, etc.

Use this site for:

- Looking for the full text of judgments from the House of Lords cases since 1996.

Court Service

The Court Service web site (**http://www.courtservice.gov.uk**) publishes on the Internet a selection of judgments from the Royal Courts of Justice. The decision whether to publish a judgment is left to the individual judge, as a consequence some courts are more heavily represented than others, in particular, there are a lot of judgments from the Technology and Construction Court. The site was launched in 1997 so some judgments are available from that date but a lot more have been put online recently. If you are looking for a recent major Court of Appeal or High Court Case you will probably find it here.

On site there is also a list of judgments recently added which can be useful and a new site specific search engine enabling searches using natural language or Boolean operators. It is also possible to search by date, court, claimant/appellant, respondent and judge.

The daily lists of all the Royal Court of Justice Courts are also available on site.

Every time I have visited the site there has been a problem with the speed of access, a lot of connections being "timed out", *i.e.* the connections between the pages are so slow that the computer gives up trying to open the page. Hopefully these problems will have been addressed by the time of publication.

Use this site for:

- Looking for recent full text judgments from the Court of Appeal, Queens Bench Division or Technology and Construction Courts.

The Incorporated Council of Law Reporting for England and Wales

The Incorporated Council of Law Reporting site (**http://www. lawreports.co.uk**) gives free access to a selection of The Councils services. The Incorporated Council of law reporting do not themselves provide an online subscription service with the full Law reports but they do provide the material for the Justis.com site (**http://www.justis.com**). This site is reviewed in the legal research section, see p. 127. The free services provided by the Incorporated Council of Law Reporting are detailed below.

The Weeklies

There is free access to case reports that are soon to appear in the Weekly Law Reports.

The Law Reports

There is only a list of cases recently reported, no actual free case reports.

Daily Law Notes

This is by far the most useful resource on this site. Daily Law Notes contains case summaries. These summaries are on the site within 24 hours of judgment. The summaries are of a uniformly high standard. The stated aim of Daily Law Notes is to provide reports of "all significant decisions of the superior courts". The intention is to only report cases that break new ground irrespective of their court. Courts covered by Daily Law Notes are the House of Lords, Courts of

Appeal, Chancery Division, Queen's Bench Division, Family Division, European Courts of Justice and other courts, including the Restrictive Practices Court.

The case summaries go back about 6–8 months in time. There are no search facilities on the site.

Use this site for:

- Finding very recent case reports before they go into The Weeklies.

- Regularly checking Daily Law Notes to keep up to date on developments in case law.

Smith Bernal

Smith Bernal are the official court reporters to the Royal Courts of Justice. They provide free and subscription services through their web site. The free service called "casebase" (**http://www.smithbernal.com**) is very much a taster to get you hooked so you will move on to their subscription service. Casebase is an archive of Court of Appeal judgments from 1996–98. To access more recent Court of Appeal judgments or judgments from other courts it is necessary to use Smith Bernals' subscription service. The subscription service is known as casetrack and details are given below.

Use this site for:

- Finding out about the services offered by Smith Bernal.

The Times Law Reports

The Times Law Reports can be accessed from the front page of *The Times* (**http://www.the-times.co.uk**), choose Law Reports for recent law reports. If you want to access reports from earlier additions there is a new search facility on site that enables you to search back to the beginning of 2000, but no further. Be aware that the search facility is general to the whole paper; take care in framing your searches. In particular, if you are looking for a case narrow down your time frame and be careful with your search words.

> I wanted to find a report of the case between the Spice Girls and Aprilia. I searched using the full case name: *Spice Girls Ltd.* v. *Aprilia World Service* BV (2000). Don't search like this in The Times Law Reports. If you do you will get hundreds of football match reports For a much more effective search substitute an "and" for the "v."

Use this site for:

- Looking for case reports from January 2000.

British and Irish Legal Information Institute

The Bailii project (**http://www.bailii.org**) is currently in its pilot phase (see p. 44 for an explanation of the aims of Bailii). But even given that it is still a very useful site gathering all in one place links to the free case reports on the Internet and providing search facilities across the sites.

Cases or links on the Bailii site at present include:

- Employment Appeal Tribunal—decisions from July 1999.
- Social Security and Child Support Commissioners—selected opinions from January 1997.
- Court of Appeal—selected judgments from January 2000.
- High Court of Justice—selected judgments from January 2000.

There are also Northern Irish, Scottish and Irish decisions as well.

When this idea comes to full fruition it will be an amazing free legal resource for law students, professionals and the public alike.

Use this site at present for:

- Finding recent Employment Appeal Tribunal decisions.
- Finding Social Security and Child Commissioners opinions from 1997.
- Finding recent selected Court of Appeal and High Court judgments.

Swarbrick and Co.

Swarbrick and Company is a firm of Yorkshire solicitors among the first on the web (**http://www.swarb.co.uk**). They maintain an extensive website. In particular, there are case summaries of important cases going back as far as 1992.

Use this site for:

- Checking out whether there are any case summaries in an area you are researching. If there are, read the summary and decide if you need to follow up and find the full judgment.

Subscription Services

Subscription services provided by online legal publishers generally offer quite a lot more than the basic legal information offered by the free sites. You are paying for the better search facilities, commentary, hyperlinking, updating and speed of delivery. There are a lot of different services on offer at varying prices. When looking for case law products or more general legal research products (see p. 111 for details) you need to establish what type of research a firm or lawyer needs to carry out and then find the product that matches these needs at the right price.

Smith Bernal

The Smith Bernal subscription service is purely case-based and is called casetrack. All judgments from the following courts are contained in the database:

- Courts of Appeal (Criminal and Civil)—1996 to present day.
- High Court judgments (Queen's Bench Division (including Crown Office List and Commercial Court), Chancery Division (including Patents Court and Revenue Court) and Employment Appeals Tribunal—from July 1998 to present day.

The service is free for academics, charities and not for profit organisations otherwise the fees vary depending on the size of the practice starting at approximately £325 per annum for a small practice up to approximately £2800 per annum.

Smith Bernal prides itself on the speed upon which it can bring judgments online—claiming a record of 26 minutes.

The search facilities enable searches by case name, date, free text, fields and subject. The intention is to be able to search for a specific transcript. It is also possible to keep up to date with new cases by scrolling through new judgments and checking out specific subject areas.

The information on search techniques is clear and concise. It would be worth printing off the general information on using connectors "and", "or" etc.) to use on other sites as well. "Less is more" is excellent advice for a lot of these sites. If you are searching for a specific case, one accurate, hopefully unusual, word from the title is more likely to get the right result than a string of common words.

There is no hyperlinking on site to other cases on the database and no information as to whether the case has been considered, applied or repealed in other cases. To find these added refinements you would need to subscribe to one of the legal publishers sites like Westlaw or Butterworths Direct.

I tried out the search facilities on casetrack to look for a case on the liability of Internet Service Providers for defamatory material posted on their service. I couldn't remember the name or date, just the fact that it was quite recent. It would have to be given the limitations on the casetrack database. I tried searching in the High Court under the sub-heading defamation but came up with far too many results. The second search tactic was to use the free text search. This is where the search engine searches for the text you choose in the whole database. It is important to frame these searches correctly and even more important to read the information on how to search on screen.

My first search was "Internet Service Provider" near defamation. This resulted in 36 hits, unfortunately this was not much use as I did not have the time to scroll through until I found the relevant case. I tried again with "Internet Service Provider" and defamation. This gave me one hit, the right case, *Godfrey (Laurence)* v. *Demon Internet Limited* 1999, QBD. This judgment is worth reading by anyone who wants to read a concise and clear explanation of Internet Service Providers, e-mail and newsgroups. The law on defamation on the Internet is interesting too.

Use this site for:

- Finding named judgments.
- Detailed legal research.

New Law Online (**http://www.cchnewlaw.co.uk**)

New Law Online is another case-based legal research service. The database of cases starts from January 1995. As well as providing the growing research database New Law also has a daily digest service, where important and relevant decisions in among others the High Court, Court of Appeal, European Court of Justice and Employment Appeal Tribunal are provided online prior to full judgment being handed down.

Other services provided by New Law include the ability to check out new transcripts as they are added to the database. It is also possible to limit your searches to particular areas of interest.

I found the real benefits of using New Law to be the indices. These indices provide a useful way of cross-referencing research. For instance, if you wanted to know what cases had considered the Dangerous Dogs Act 1991. Choose statutes from the index list, then choose the letter D from the alphabet, scroll down until you find the correct Act and click. You will find displayed in the left-hand frame all the cases on the database which have considered this piece of legislation. The same process can be carried out for several different categories including statutory instruments, courts, counsel, E.U. and international material.

Another useful feature of New Law is the personal alert service, a service increasingly being offered. The New Law system enables you to choose the search you want to be made and then when a case comes online that satisfies the search criteria you will be notified by e-mail and through the personal alert service on the New Law site. Both methods providing a direct link to the case.

The added features on New Law I found very good and the searching was relatively straightforward.

> My research involved the Dangerous Dogs Act and particularly whether any court had defined the meaning of section 10(3) 'dangerously out of control'. Using the index search I was able to home in very quickly on one recent relevant case, *Rafiq* v. *DPP* 1997. No judgment was available online but I was able to read the case summary and to review other cases on the Dangerous Dogs Act 1991.

One criticism I would make is the lack of hyperlinking between cases on the database. Another area where there is room for improvement is the way information is presented on screen. I found it difficult to read and I had to constantly adjust the screen to make the information easier to read.

New Law subscriptions start at approximately £600 per annum for two users.

Use this site for:

- Finding named case reports.
- Detailed legal research.

Government Publications

All lawyers need to look at government publications sometimes. Whether it is for student research on environmental law at the department of the environment site, a lawyer in practice looking for the report from the Stephen Lawrence enquiry or for checking out the amendments to the civil procedure rules, government documents are an essential resource for all lawyers.

Government publications were in the past extremely difficult to find. Published by different departments or by HMSO it was often a case of where do I start looking not where can I find it. The situation has improved due to the advent of the Internet and the commitment of the government. The Internet has made it possible to navigate the corridors of power, obscure reports previously only available to the very few are suddenly available at the click of the mouse. The government has also invested time and money in putting government on the Internet. The plan is that all government services will be accessible on the Internet by 2008. The open government site (**http://www.open.gov.uk**) is an excellent starting point. It is essentially an index of all government sites on the Internet with direct links to the site you are looking for. Otherwise the most useful site is the Lord Chancellors' (**http://www.open.gov.uk/lcd**) with the new civil procedure rules.

Open Government Site

Whether you are looking for the Ministry of Defence or the Commission for Racial Equality the simplest way to start your search is to go to the open government site (**http://www.open.gov.uk**). The site lists government departments, local authorities, police forces, the Benefits Agency, the Child Support Agency, Companies house, the Church of England, the monarchy and hundreds of other government and public bodies. Searches can be by topic or alphabetically by organisation. When you locate the relevant ministry, department or organisation link to their web site by clicking on their name. From that point it is often quite simple to find the paper or report required by following links. If you cannot find the document you are looking for use the contact details on site to e-mail the appropriate person or telephone them.

Use this site:

• As a starting point when looking for government materials.

The Stationery Office

The Stationery Office is the privatised arm of HMSO. It is now charged with the responsibility of publishing a lot of official government information. The Stationery Office has more than one web site. Its consumer friendly "its official" site (**http://www.itsofficial.co.uk**) was at the time of writing partially under construction. It appeared that the site was very much aimed at the consumer and not the legal professional. Of far more use was the Stationery Offices official documents site (**http://www.official-documents.co.uk**). This site is host to U.K. official publications on the Internet here it was possible to browse through all Stationery Office publications by date, title or department. Publications available include Command Papers, public inquiries and budgets going back to 1994 and a lot more. Other official publications on the Internet, not published by the Stationery Office like Hansard, Law Commission Reports and consultative documents are also on site. Search facilities including the use of Boolean operators are available.

The Stationery Office also publishes the daily list of government publications (**http://www.the-stationery-office.co.uk**) and at another Stationery Office site (**http://www.ukop.co.uk**) a full list of all British official publications from 1980 to the present, this list includes publications not available online. This site is subscription only.

Use the Stationery Office sites:

- To find Command Papers and other government reports.
- To find official publications published from 1980 onwards.
- To look up the daily list.

Inforoute

A new government site hosted by HMSO (**http://www.hmso.gov.uk/ inforoute**) is Inforoute. This web site is designed to act as a gateway and central information point for official government information. It is linked in with the governments plan for each government department to set up an Information Asset Register (IAR). These IARs would contain all the government information for a department including previously unpublished reports, statistics and data. The plan is that through Inforoute all the information on the department IARs will be made available to the public for the first time. The project is up and running at the moment but is far from complete. There is a search engine on site that hopefully is good enough to cope with the huge volume of information soon to be available.

When this site is fully developed use it:

- For detailed research using government reports and statistics.

The London Gazette

Another useful resource is *The London Gazette* (**http://www. londongazette.co.uk**). It is possible to view the last two issues free online and others with a subscription. The information is well presented and it is simple to check what the government has recently published.

Use this site:

- To check on recent government publications.

The Badger Alerter

The Badger Alerter is a daily service free from Sweet and Maxwell (**http://www.sweetandmaxwell.co.uk**) detailing new developments in law, regulation and compliance. A useful site worth bookmarking if you want to keep up to date.

Use this site:

- For keeping up to date on new law and regulations published by the government.

Lord Chancellors Department: The Woolf Reforms

An essential site for all litigators is the Lord Chancellor's department site (**http://www.open.gov.uk/lcd/**) where the civil procedure rules and practice directions can be found. Not the official source, that is still the Stationery Office publication of the rules, but the Lord Chancellor's web site is where all practitioners turn to check out a rule or new practice direction. The material on the site can be downloaded but as is often the case it is in perfect document format (pdf). This is a method of storing information on a computer. Files that are stored in this way are unreadable unless you have the correct software to act as a translator. The most commonly found software needed to translate this type of file is called Adobe Acrobat Reader software. It is possible to download this from a link on the Lord Chancellor's site or alternatively download from the Adobe site (**http://www. adobe.com**). In addition, it is also necessary to unzip some files when downloaded on to your computer as some of the information is stored on site in a zipped format. See p. 27 for information on zipping and unzipping and how to obtain the software needed.

The rules, practice directions and protocols on site are well set out and easy to find.

Use this site:

- As a source of a complete up to date set of the civil procedure rules and practice directions.

Woolf Commentaries

Several websites have sprung up offering commentary on the Woolf Reforms. I have looked at a few of the free services.

Beagle

The Beagle site (**http://www.beagle.org.uk/cpr**) is probably the best known of the Woolf sites. The beagle, now known to be HHJ Overend, has done a very good job of making the detailed rules, directions and protocols easy to follow. In particular, you can look at any rule and see immediately if there is a practice direction associated with it and then link to it. There are full search facilities on site. The site is not really about commentary but more about presenting the material in a clear structured manner. To download you need to unzip the files so you will need some unzipping software. See p. 27 for information on zipping and unzipping.

Lawonline

The Woolf in practice pages at Lawonline (**http://www.lawonline.cc**) are part of Laurie West-Knights web site. To access the Woolf pages, a password is needed. In order to get a password you will need to e-mail Laurie West-Knights with an explanation of who you are, why you are there and why you want access. It is actually a simpler process than it sounds and although you need a password, access is free. Once you have registered and received your username and password you can access the site where you will find an up to date detailed commentary on the rules. New material is highlighted with commentary and links to the rules, statutory instruments and other sites. These pages presume a detailed knowledge of the litigation process and are therefore not for the beginner but are of great use to the experienced litigator trying to keep up with the constant change.

Simmons and Simmons

If it was up to date the Simmons and Simmons site would be a good basic introduction to the Woolf reforms. The site consists of simple easy to follow commentary with a link to the rules themselves. But when I looked at it the site had not been updated for six months!

2 Temple Gardens

Another commentary site which was quite easy to follow was the 2 Temple Gardens site (**http://2templegardens.co.uk/woolf/1Index. htm**). This time it was not clear whether this site was up to date or not as I couldn't find an easily visible "last updated" note.

YAWS

A rather different site is Roger Hornes "Yet Another Woolf Site" or YAWS (**http://www.number7.demon.co.uk**). This site uses automated hyperlinking to cross-reference between rules and practice directions. So, whenever one rule mentions another an automatic hyperlink is created. This is very clever and will undoubtedly be how a lot of web publishing will be done in the future. Unfortunately, maybe it was a bad day or my browser is just not up to it but on my screen YAWS did not work. Give it a try and see if it is just me.

Choose one of these sites:

- To give you commentary on the rules.
- To keep you up to date on amendments to the rules.
- To keep you informed of new practice directions.

10 Downing Street

To complete your tour of government web sites if you really feel the need you can visit, the Prime Minister, Tony Blair at his web site (**http://www.10downingstreet.gov.uk**).

Parliamentary Publications

The majority of lawyers and law students research the law at times by studying an Act of Parliament. Sometimes it is necessary to go a step further and find out why a particular section was drafted as it was or what questions have been put to the House on a particular topic. Luckily for all lawyers, Parliament is well and truly on the Internet. *Hansard*, Public Bills, standing committee debates, written questions, orders of business, it is all there. Even if you want to find out how much money the House of Commons made (or lost) on refreshments or which Member of Parliament has a complimentary membership to Stringfellows look to Parliament's web site (**http://www. parliament.uk**). This web site is the best place to start for the majority of parliamentary materials. The site is quite straightforward and simple with no flash graphics but all the better for it. Of all the information available the full debates in *Hansard* are a particularly useful and fascinating resource. Unless specified otherwise all references in this section are to the parliament site.

If you cannot find the disco mad M.P., the answer and how to find him is at the end of this section.

The Houses of Parliament

This section is going to focus initially on parliamentary materials common to both Houses that are neither legislative nor caselaw. Legislation on the parliament site is covered in the section on legislation, see p. 46 and House of Lords case law is covered in the section on case law, see p. 47. Then this section will look at the materials specific to each House, concluding with the daily list site.

Parliamentary Materials Common to both Houses

Hansard

Hansard on the Internet is available from parliamentary session 1993–94. There are ongoing plans to put earlier editions online but no timetable is available yet.

The debates are clearly set out and easily accessible. The previous days debates are posted at 9.00 a.m. the following morning.

To find *Hansard* follow the links to either the House of Commons or the House of Lords and choose publications on the Internet and then *Hansard* or if you are looking for a specific debate, question or M.P.'s contributions use the search facilities.

Use this site for:

• Detailed research on public policy and issues behind government proposals and legislation.

Command Papers

Command Papers are an important category of parliamentary papers not generally to be found on the parliament site but are scattered around among a whole range of sites. Command Papers include the majority of government and law commission reports, reports of Royal Commissions and White Papers. As stated above Command Papers can be found in a lot of places. For instance, law commission reports can be found at the law commission site (**http://www.open.gov.uk/ lawcomm/hompage.htm**) and government reports at the sites of individual government departments, find them using the open government site (**http://www.open.gov.uk**). Alternatively, as Command Papers are official documents a selection can be found at the Stationery Office official document site (**http://www.official-documents.co.uk**). Choose the "official publications on the Internet" to link to a list which includes Command Papers. Those available are listed alphabetically by title and date from 1996, though there is only a selection on site. Alternatively, there are search facilities that use natural language or Boolean operators.

I have yet to find a full searchable list of Command Papers anywhere on the Internet, a search would have to be using the Stationery Office official documents site and then if the document was not available there search the government department site, otherwise it is back to the law library.

Use these sites for:

- Finding Command Papers.

- In-depth research on the issues covered.

- Updating on government thinking in the area of the report.

- Finding out about new proposals for law reform in the law commission reports.

Public Bills before Parliament

Tracking the progress of a Bill through Parliament is relatively easy. Choosing: (1) either House; (2) publications on the Internet; and (3) Public Bills will bring you to the relevant pages. On these pages are a list of all the Bills now before parliament. Bills before the House of Commons are marked with a green diamond and those before the House of Lords a red diamond. At the head of each Bill is a note stating the stage the Bill has reached in its passage through parliament. Amendments proposed are also to be found under each Bill. The full text of the Bill as it currently stands can be browsed.

Alternatively, a complete list and text of Public Bills introduced in the current session can be found in the weekly information bulletin, a link being provided on site. The weekly information bulletin has Bills for sessions from the 1997/8 session onwards.

Use this site for:

- Tracking the progress of Bills before parliament.

The House of Commons

Debates

The five most recent editions of the House of Commons debates are available for browsing online otherwise it is necessary to use the search facilities. The standing committee debates on Bills are listed by the title of the Bill being considered and are available from the 1997–98 session. Other standing committee debates, for instance, the standing committee on delegated legislation is also available from the 1997–98 session and can be browsed by choosing the relevant committee.

House of Commons Papers

Papers relevant to the proceedings in the House can be found on the House of Commons pages. These include early day motions, questions for oral or written answer, orders of business, statutory instruments, European Community documents considered by the House and hidden away in "other House of Commons papers", the register of members interests which makes fascinating reading.

Use these sites for:

- In-depth research on government and opposition policy and thinking.

The House of Lords

Debates

The five most recent editions of debates in the House of Lords are available on the pages to browse. Otherwise the House of Lords pages allow searching by category. So, it is possible to search a debate on a specific Bill or on a specific piece of delegated legislation or by the heading of the debate or the name of the committee.

In addition the parliamentary site search engine searches *Hansard* as well as other publications on site. The searches are in natural language or using Boolean operators. Searches can also be made by specifying the name of the speaker or the number of a parliamentary question you wish to find.

House of Lords Papers

House of Lords papers are more limited but minutes and Order Papers are on site and details of the select committee's sitting and the full text of some select committee reports. The Register of Lords interests is there too.

Use the sites for:

- In-depth research on government and opposition thinking and policy.

The Daily List

The Daily List published by The Stationery Office at one of their numerous websites (**http://www.the-stationery-office.co.uk**) is a list of all parliamentary and official non-parliamentary publications published on a specific day. Publication and ordering details are provided.

Use this site for:

- Checking what parliamentary publications have been published.

(If anyone is interested the M.P. with a complimentary membership to Stringfellows is Nigel Evans M.P. (Ribble Valley). Search using "Stringfellows". A page referring to the Register of Members interests comes up, open page and scroll down to Nigel Evans).

European Union Law

Even if you are not a specialist in European law it will have an impact on your daily practice and there will be times when you will need to find a new case from the European Court of Justice or a Regulation. If you are studying law you will probably already have used some of the sources listed below for research but hopefully there will be some new sources you haven't yet come across.

I have started my tour of the E.U. web sites with the Europa site. Europa is the official information server of the E.U. (**http:// www.europa.eu.int**). The Europa site is available in 11 languages and is the best place to start any tour of the E.U. sites and should be bookmarked if you ever need to research E.U. law on the Internet. Europa is in the process of being updated. A lot of the site was under construction at the time of writing and so if parts haven't been reviewed it is because they were not available or were just about to be replaced.

I have then broken the sites down into institutional sites, general European law sites and then specific sites for treaties, legislation and case law. I have concluded by looking at a range of other E.U. sites that may be useful for research or practice.

Apart from the Europa site another site worth bookmarking if finding E.U. law is something you need to do regularly is the SCAD site (**http://europa.eu.int/scad**) (see below).

It should be noted that a lot of the documents, legislation and treaties are available in pdf, see p. 58 for details of where the necessary software can be downloaded.

Search Tip

On each of the different Europa sites you will see tucked away in a corner the European flag and Europa symbol. One click on the Europa symbol will take you back to the home page of Europa from where you can link to other sites.

The Europa Homepage

The Europa homepage is divided into four main sections providing links to the following:

- News: press releases, calendar of upcoming events, official Euro rates and other news services.
- Abc: Basic information on the E.U., citizens rights, access to official documents, publications and databases and sources of information.
- Institutions: parliament, council, commission, court of justice, court of auditors, economic and social committee, committee of the regions, European investment bank, European central bank and other bodies.
- Policies: Access by subject to legal instruments in force, legislative activity, implementation of common policy, E.U. grants and loans, statistic and publications.

Use this site for:

- Accessing other sites in the Europa database.

The Institutions of the European Union

All the institutions of the E.U. can be accessed through the Europa homepage (**http://www.europa.eu.int**) or their own homepages. Taking each of the institutions in turn I have set out below the facilities provided on their web pages. The most useful site for lawyers will almost certainly be the European Court of Justice site.

The Council of the European Union

The Council homepage (**http://ue.eu.int/en/main.htm**) provides information about the role of the council, who sits on the council, timetables of meetings as well as more substantive information on the policies of the E.U.

There are links to the treaties and governments online.

Use this site for:

- Finding out about the role and composition of the Council.

The European Commission

The European Commission homepage (**http://europa.eu.int/comm/ index_en.htm**) provides links to information on the role of the Commission, the reform of the Commission as well as profiles of the 20 current commissioners. Romano Prodi, the current president of the Commission, even has his own homepage. There are links to Green and White Policy Papers published by the Commission since 1984 and Commission Reports.

Use this site for:

- Finding out about the role and composition of the Commission.
- Researching Commission policy.

The European Court of Justice and Court of First Instance

The European Court of Justice homepage (**http://europa.eu.int/cj**) contains a lot of information on the court, its jurisdiction, procedure and members. A lot of the web site was still under construction at the time of writing so it is difficult to evaluate how useful it will be for research purposes. Functions on the web site include a recent case law function providing the full text of recent cases before the European Court of Justice and the Court of First Instance. There are some important and helpful notes on the correct citation of articles of the treaties pre-and post-Amsterdam Treaty.

The rules of procedure of the courts can be found under texts relating to the institutions. The research and documentation area will include an alphabetical and numerical list of cases that have been before the Court of Justice. There is no text of the cases here. The Digest of Community case law will at some stage have summaries of judgments and orders of the European Court of Justice. There will also be an alphabetical index of legal issues. As most of the site is under construction it is not possible to say what search facilities will be available. I am informed that the intention is to put all the cases of the Court of Justice on the web site but that it is not possible to give a date for completion as it is a very complex task! This also seems to go against the stated aim of creating one large database of European Law with the proposed merging of the Eur-Lex, Celex and Eudor sites (see below). For access to E.U. case law at the present time see the Eur-Lex site at **http://europa.eu.int/eur-lex** reviewed below.

Use the ECJ site (when it is completed) for:

- Finding ECJ judgments.
- Researching E.U. case law.
- Learning about the Rules of Procedure of the European Court of Justice and the Court of First Instance.
- Finding out about the correct citation of articles of the treaties.

The European Parliament

The European Parliament homepage (**http://www.europarl.eu.int**) contains a lot of information about the European Parliament including details on the parliamentary committees and parliamentary questions.

There are links to the European treaties (pdf, see p. 58), Com documents (Commission proposals and communications) and the official journals.

Use this site for:

- Finding out about the function of the European Parliament.

European Union Law

In Spring 2001 the databases of Eur-Lex, Celex and Eudor are to be unified and a single database of European law will be available, with limited free access and subscription services accessible from one site. But currently three separate sites exist. The two subscription sites Celex and Eudor and the free Europa site, Eur-Lex.

Celex

The official database for European law is Celex (**http://europa.eu.int/celex**). This is a subscription service with payment either annually or per search. The annual cost for unlimited access is 960 euros per annum with an alternative pay as you go option of 0.2 euros per document. The service is aimed mainly at professionals and European officials and provides a very comprehensive database of European law and quite user friendly search facilities.

Eur-lex

Alternatively, a large amount of European law is accessible through the Europa server and particularly the Eur-Lex service provided by the Commission (**http://europa.eu.int/eur-lex**). Eur-Lex gives free access to the treaties, the consolidated legislation database, case law of the European Court of Justice and the Court of First Instance and the full text of the Official Journal for the current 45 days.

Eudor

A service of the Eur-Op, Office for Publications. Eudor (**http://eudor.eur-op.eu.int**) is a subscription document delivery system. The cost is 0.3 euros per document. It is intended to offer simpler access to the L and C series of the Official Journal. It is also the electronic archive of official documents of the E.U.

Use these sites for:

- Researching E.U. law.
- Finding specific cases, regulations and directives.

The following section looks in more detail at the three arms of E.U. law: the treaties, legislation and case law and more particularly where they can be found for free or otherwise on the web. The Daily Notes on the Incorporated Council of Law Reporting site are a good bookmark if you need to keep up to date with developments in this area.

European Treaties

Consolidated versions of the Treaty on European Union and the treaty establishing the European Community, incorporating changes made by the Treaty of Amsterdam are available at the Eur-lex site (**http://europa.eu.int/eur-lex/en/index.html**). Alternatively, these treaties and the Single European Act, the treaty establishing the European Coal and Steel Community and the treaty establishing the European Atomic Energy Community can be found at: **http://europa.eu.int/abc/obj/treaties/en/entoc.html**. Full text versions of all the European treaties are available from the Celex and Eudor sites.

Use these sites for:

• Locating the full text of the treaties that form the foundations of the E.U.

European Union Legislation

The full text of E.U. legislation currently in force can be accessed through Eur-lex (**http://europa.eu.int/eur-lex**). The "Community legislation in force" section contains the texts of all the legislation that has been adopted to date. The search facilities on the site allow searches by subject matter either through broad categories, "analytical structure" in eurospeak or alphabetically through subject matter. Alternatively, by pressing the search button it is possible to search either by document number if you know it, or by entering words and phrases. I found the search facilities to be slow but then there is a lot of law to search through.

Use this site for:

• Finding and researching E.U. legislation.

European Union Case Law

Eur-Lex

European Court of Justice and the Court of First Instance decisions can be found through Eur-Lex (**http://europa.eu.int/eur-lex**). Cases reported on the site date from June 17, 1997. Eur-lex states that they do not intend to post cases pre-1997 on the site but, as stated above, the Court of Justice site does intend to post all European Court of Justice cases on their site at some time in the future. It should also be noted that it takes up to two months for a new case to appear on the site.

It is possible to search the Eur-lex site by case number, dates, parties, subject matter and text. The more information you have on a case the better the search result.

Use this site for:

• Finding recent European Court of Justice judgments (but not too recent).

Incorporated Council of Law Reporting for England and Wales: Daily Law Notes: European Judgments (**http://www.lawreports.co.uk**).

The Incorporated Council of Law Reporting, Daily Law Notes are a very useful and accessible resource for recent judgments of the Courts of the European Communities. The database is updated daily. It contains summarised reports of the most important cases going back approximately six months. If you want the full report you would need to use the fee paying service. There are no search facilities on the site, but if you know what you are looking for it is a very simple way to access important European Court of Justice judgments.

Use this site for:

- Keeping up to date with developments in E.U. case law.

Other European Links

The majority of sites dealt with so far have been official sites. The following sites are an assortment of potentially useful European law sites for the student and the professional. Some are official European sites like SCAD others compilations of European links that may prove interesting to browse.

SCAD

SCAD (**http://europa.eu.int/scad**) is the bibliographic database of the European Commission library. It is essentially an index to the official documents of the European Institutions. It will not provide you with the text of the directive or the regulation you are looking for but it will give you all the details and references to enable you to find it. It has a straightforward and effective search facility and is a very useful resource.

Use this site for:

- Finding the information you need to make an effective search for any official E.U. document.

SCADPLUS

SCADPLUS (**http://europa.eu.int/scadplus**) is an extension of the SCAD database. It contains a lot of useful information about E.U. policy and includes details of national legislation and implementing directives. It is therefore possible to go to the SCADPLUS database and research the law on a particular subject matter. For instance if you needed to research the U.K.'s implementation of E.U. policy on equal opportunities. You would choose equal opportunity from the policy menu. This would link you to a screen giving links to all the relevant law including legislation in force, national implementing measures, legislation in the pipeline and recent Court of Justice law. It is also possible to access the SCADPLUS database and research policy issues from the policies section of the Europa homepage (**http://europa.eu.int**).

Use this site for:

- Researching law and policy in the E.U.
- Researching member states implementation of E.U. law.

Governments Online

The Governments Online database is a web site providing basic information about the governments of all the member states and other European countries. There are links provided to more detailed information on each country. The U.K. link is to the Foreign and Commonwealth Office site. The Governments Online web site can be found at: **http://europa.eu.int/gonline**.

Use this site for:

- Filling in the gaps from your geography lessons.
- Finding out about the government and constitutional arrangements of the member states.

European Online Dictionary

The European online dictionary (**http://www2.echo.lu/cgi/edic/Euro DicWWW.pl**) is a clever idea. It can provide you with an instant translation from any E.U. language into any other E.U. language. It can be quite slow so don't expect to translate a whole case from German to Danish in an afternoon. Choose law in the "filter on any subject" box to get accurate results.

Use this site for:

- Translating that difficult phrase into Finnish or any other E.U. language.

IDEA

IDEA (**http://europa.eu.int/idea/ideaen.html**) is an electronic database of the European institutions. It enables you to obtain contact details for persons or organizations within the E.U.

Use this site for:

- Obtaining contact details of officials working for the E.U. or any organization of the E.U.

The next two sites are two of the many portal sites for European law. They are both packed with links to European sites of interest and would be most useful if you wanted to research the E.U. on the Internet in greater depth.

European Union Internet Resources

This is a site produced by the University of Berkeley in California (**http://www.lib.berkeley.edu/GSSI/eu.html**). It is packed with links to E.U. sites.

European Information

Exeter University's site (**http://www.ex.ac.uk/~pcovery/lib/euro studies.html**) provides a really comprehensive set of links to law and information on the E.U.

International Law

A lot of international law and international institution sites are not going to be available on the Westlaw, Lawtel, Lexis or Butterworths package used in the office. Using the Internet is often the only option when looking for international materials.

Most lawyers in the U.K. don't need to find international law everyday. But for a lot of lawyers and law students there will be the occasional time when they need to find some international law or research the law of another jurisdiction. It could be because they have a cross border case and need to research the Irish Constitution or look at U.S. case law on privacy on the Internet to check on developments. Even if the country or area of law to be researched is not specifically covered in this section there should be sufficient information included for you to know where to look.

It has never been easier to research international law. It is now possible to look up international treaties, case law and the law of a lot of other jurisdictions. Like the Internet as a whole the approach is not unified and you need to know your way around but once you have found those sites that are relevant to your area of work or study the Internet is an invaluable resource. But, as ever, be aware of the source of the material. The full text of a treaty from the United Nations or Council of Europe is likely to be accurate and complete but more care needs to be taken with material from an unknown organisation.

This section is divided up into parts. The first part deals with finding: international treaties on the web, international courts and case law, international organisations and concludes with a section on sites that contain links to international law. The second part looks at the law of other jurisdictions focusing on: Scotland, Wales, Northern Ireland, Ireland and the United States of America.

Highlights would include the Avalon Project site. A huge database of hyperlinked documents including a large number of multi-lateral treaties. Another impressive site is the U.S. portal FindLaw. If you need to find law from the USA it will usually be the best place to start. Otherwise the Council of Europe maintains an excellent site with the full text of a large number of European conventions and agreements.

Treaties

United Nations Treaty Series

The United Nation Treaty series is a collection of over 34,000 treaties and international agreements (**http://untreaty.un.org**). The treaty series includes the full text of treaties from 1946 to December 1992. From December 1992 until April 1998 there are references to treaties made between these dates. The service was free until March 2000. It has now been decided to impose an annual fee of between $250 and $1000 for access to the database.

It is possible to view the treaties by country or date and also to use the search facilities. Searches can be either basic or advanced. An advanced search enables you to select more detailed parameters for your search. The search facilities work well and it is quite straightforward to find the treaty you are searching for.

If you need a more recent treaty there is also a database of recently deposited multilateral treaties (**http://untreaty.un,org/ENGLISH/ notpub/notpubl.asp**). These are treaties not yet published in the UN Treaty Series but the full text is published here. The treaties on this site tend to appear about one month after publication. The search facilities for the treaty series do not extend to treaties recently deposited. The only way to find the appropriate treaty is to scroll through a very long list.

Use this subscription site for:

- In-depth research into international treaties.

Foreign and Commonwealth Office

The Foreign and Commonwealth Office site (**http://www.fco.gov/ directory**) provides a list of all the treaties deposited with the U.K. but with no text available. There are contact details on the site to a Treaty Enquiry Service at the Foreign Office.

Since January 1997 explanatory memoranda must accompany all treaties to which the U.K. intends to accede. These explanatory memoranda set out among other things the subject matter of the treaty and policy considerations. These memoranda, unlike the actual treaties are accessible from the Foreign and Commonwealth Office site. It is not possible to use the search facilities on site to search for explanatory memoranda as searching is confined to the news archive. To find the relevant explanatory memoranda on this site it is necessary to scroll through a long and ever increasing list. Or, alternatively, as explanatory memoranda are Command Papers a search can be done through the Stationery Office site (**http:// www.official-documents.co.uk**).

Use this site for:

- Contact details for the Foreign and Commonwealth Office Treaty Service.

- To research government policy on treaty matters by reading the explanatory memoranda.

The Avalon Project

Yale University have put together an impressive and expansive site of law, government, diplomatic and historical documents (**http:// elsinore.cis.yale.edu/lawweb/avalon/20th/.htm**). The purpose of the project is to collect and publish on the Internet primary source materials in these areas from pre-eighteenth century to the present day. There are a large number of international treaties on site including a collection of U.S. multilateral treaties (1864–1999) as well as a lot of European treaties. A useful feature is the presence of hyperlinks to other texts referred to in the document. There are search facilities on site. If you are looking for an obscure legal document or treaty this would be a good place to start.

Use this site for:

- Finding and researching U.S., European and international treaties.

Multilaterals Project at Tufts University

The Fletcher School of Law and Diplomacy at Tufts University, a well respected institution, hosts the web site of the multilaterals project. The project, started in 1992, is designed to make available on the web international multilateral conventions and other instruments. The web site (**http://www.tufts.edu/fletcher/multilaterals.html**) is not a comprehensive set of international multilateral treaties but it does contain the full text of a large number of treaties made in the second half of this century and quite a few from earlier times. It is possible to search for treaties by category or by using the search facilities on the site. Given the recent introduction of fee charging for access to the UN Treaty Series this site is now an even more important resource.

Use this site for:

- Finding and researching international multilateral treaties.

HMSO

The text of some bilateral treaties entered into by the U.K. from 1997 onwards can be found on the HMSO web site (**http:// www.hmso.gov.uk**). The bilateral treaties that are available on this site are those scheduled to Orders in Council for their implementation. In simple terms if the treaty is brought into force by way of Order in Council and the treaty is annexed to the Order in Council as a schedule then you will find it on this web site. To find the treaties on the web site you will need to search statutory instruments by a number or word search. By searching for double taxation I came up with the full text of numerous double taxation treaties entered into by the U.K. since 1997.

Use this site for:

• Finding U.K. bilateral treaties.

Stationery Office Site

The Stationery Office (**http://www.the-stationery-office.co.uk**) does not publish the U.K. treaty series as a complete collection but all those published since 1996 onwards are available and those published earlier can be obtained from them by mail order.

Use this site for:

• Finding and researching recent U.K. treaties.

Council of Europe

The Council of Europe has an excellent site. A complete set of the texts of European conventions and agreements signed or ratified within the framework of the Council of Europe is available and searchable (**http://conventions.coe.int**). The European Treaty Series can be searched by category, say, human rights or public law or by a text search. The site has a "what's new" button. This gives details of the countries that have recently ratified European conventions. It is also possible to check by country which treaties have been signed or ratified and when.

Use this site for:

• Finding and researching treaties in the European Treaty Series.
• Finding and researching European conventions.

International Courts and Case Law

International Court of Justice

The International Court of Justice sits at The Hague and decides disputes in accordance with international law. The web site (**http://www.icj-cij.org**) sets out the role, history, composition and jurisdiction of the court. There are links to the docket of cases pending before the court and to the decisions and advisory opinions of the court. The decisions are listed in reverse chronological order since 1946. There is also a page with contentious cases such as: Yugoslavia v. United Kingdom, Legality Use of Force, listed chronologically by country. The full text of all the judgments are given. There are search facilities on site, which allow a basic text search of your choice of documents and a more advanced search facility. It is also possible to order publications from the site.

Use this site for:

• Finding and reading the decisions and opinions of the court.

European Court of Human Rights

The European Court of Human Rights was set up in 1959 by the Council of Europe to deal with alleged violations of the European Convention on Human Rights (1950). In 1998 a full time court was established. The court has a basic but effective web site (**http://www.echr.coe.int**). Details are given of the composition, history and organisation of the court. The European Convention on Human Rights is reproduced in full and full text of all judgments and court opinions on the admissibility of cases are available. There are good search facilities enabling text searches or searches by title, parties, application number, etc. A useful extra is the list of press releases; the majority announce a recent judgment and give a summary of the case. They act very much like a detailed headnote and as such it is a good idea to look at the press release before deciding whether you need to read the full judgment.

Use this site for:

• Finding the full text of The European Convention of Human Rights.

• Reading the full text of judgments of the court.

- Keeping up to date with new cases by reading the press releases with case summaries on site.

International Criminal Court

The International Criminal Court (**http://www.un.org/law/icc/index.htm**) has yet to come into existence. The web site sets out the jurisdiction and status of the UN sponsored International Criminal Court. The court will come into being when 60 states have ratified the treaty. The court will have jurisdiction over genocide, crimes against humanity and war crimes.

Use this site for:

- Nothing much at the moment, but it is interesting to read about the proposals for and jurisdiction of the proposed court.

International Tribunal for Law of the Sea

The International Tribunal for Law of the Sea (**http://www.un.org/ depts/los/index.htm**) is a tribunal set up under the auspices of the United Nations Convention on the Law of the Sea (1982). Its function is to settle disputes concerning the interpretation and application of the convention. The tribunal based in Hamburg came into force in November 1994. The web site gives details of the jurisdiction and work of the tribunal as well as case transcripts to all the cases and relevant documents and recommendations.

Use this site for:

- Finding out about the ITLOS.
- Reading case transcripts.

International Organisations

United Nations

The UN has a major presence on the web, its homepage (**http:// www.un.org**) provides links to information about the UN, UN publications, UN organisations, international law and human rights. The index button takes you to a full index of links to all areas of the site.

Use this site for:

- Finding out about the UN.
- Linking to other UN organisations.

Council of Europe

The Council of Europe is an international organisation based in Strasbourg in France. Its role is to strengthen democracy and human rights and the rule of law throughout its member states. There are currently 41 member states. The web site (**http://www.coe.fr/index.asp**) has details about the establishment of the Council of Europe and links to the councils institutions: the parliamentary assembly, committee of ministers and congress of local regional authorities. There is also a link to the human rights site (**http://www.dhdirhr.coe.fr**).

Use this site for:

- Finding out about the Council of Europe.
- Linking to the human rights site.

United Nations Commission on International Trade Law

UNCITRAL is an organisation set up by the UN to formulate international trade law. The web site (**http://www.uncitral.org**) sets out details of the functions of UNCITRAL. The full text of conventions, Model laws and other texts are available. Searches of the conventions and Model laws are by subject area only. Court decisions and arbitrations relating to the conventions and Model laws are collected together on site, specifically court decisions that interpret or apply a specific provision or provisions or relate to a legal text in general. A search facility of "Case Law on UNCITRAL Texts (CLOUT)" is available.

Use this site for:

- Finding and researching international trade conventions and Model laws.
- Finding case law that interprets and applies the Model laws.

World Trade Organisation

The World Trade Organisation based in Geneva was established in 1995. It currently has 135 members. Its functions, among others, are to administer the World Trade Agreements, be a forum for trade negotiations and to settle disputes. The web site (**http://www.wto.org/wto**) has a lot of information about the policies and aims of the World Trade Organisation with sections on each major area of trade; goods, services, intellectual property, etc. Legal texts on the site include the texts for the Uruguay Round Agreements 1986–94. There is also a detailed explanation of the disputes procedure but no details of actual disputes before the World Trade Organisation.

Use this site for:

- Finding out about the World Trade Organisation.
- Looking up legal texts on World Trade Organisation issues.

International Links

Having looked at a variety of international law sites and sites for international organisations it is still likely that at times you may need to find law from another jurisdiction or international law that has not been covered by the above. In order to do this the easiest approach is to find a good set of international law links and research the law in question with this as your starting point. I have therefore included below a selection of sites with international law links.

Indiana Law School

In 1992 the Indiana University School of Law at Bloomington was chosen by CERN, the originators of the World Wide Web to host the Virtual Law Library (**http://www.law.indiana.edu/law/v-lib/lawindex.html**). The site is organized into subject related web sites maintained by institutions throughout the world. Following the international links will bring you to an extensive list of countries and resources. Whether you are interested in a Journal of African Law or decisions of Germany's Constitutional Court it is all to be found here.

Use this site for:

- Your starting point if you are researching law of other jurisdictions.

MacRoberts

The Glaswegian solicitor's site (**http://www.macroberts.co.uk**) has an extensive set of international links. Choose the legal resources button to take you to a table of links to countries from Andorra to Greece. There are also other useful legal links to other Scottish and English sites.

Use this site for:

• Researching the law of other jurisdictions.

Foreign and International Law Library at the University of Houston

The Foreign and International Law library site (**http://www.law.uh. edu/librarians/mulligan/foreignlaw**) is an eclectic selection of international primary law sources from Albania to Zambia. It is just another example showing how law librarians, in this case Timothy Mulligan, have led the way with innovative legal web sites.

Use this site for:

• Finding the law of other jurisdictions.

Other Jurisdictions

This book would not be complete without including details of web sites from neighbouring jurisdictions both as a service to lawyers in those jurisdictions and as a help to lawyers in England and Wales. I have also included a section on the USA because it is often important for European lawyers to know what the important legal developments are in America. America is in many ways ahead of Europe (and in some ways behind) in their development of the Internet as a tool for lawyers.

Scotland

The Scottish legal world is well served by the Internet. The Scottish Court web site has quite a large selection of cases on site and the Scottish parliament site is easy to use and will eventually have a large body of law on site.

British and Irish Legal Information Institute

The Bailii Project (**http://www.bailii.org**) web site will in time have Scottish case law and statutes on site. At the moment, as the project is in the pilot phase, there is currently the following case law:

- Court of Session Opinions—from September 1998, and opinions in commercial cases—from January 1998.

- Scottish High Court of Judiciary-Criminal opinions—from December 1997.

It is intended that fully searchable and hyperlinked Scottish statutes and statutory instruments will be on site. At the moment there is a search engine on site capable of searching the cases that are there.

Legislation

Primary
The majority of legislation affecting Scotland will be found at Her Majesty's Stationery Office site (**http://www.hmso.gov.uk**) under U.K. Parliament. The links to Scottish Parliament take you to legislation passed by the Scottish Parliament. At the time of writing there were two Acts! There are search facilities on site these will obviously become more useful as the site develops. Like Acts of the U.K. Parliament, the Scottish Acts appear as originally passed by Parliament, *i.e.* without amendments or even showing which provisions have come into force. It appears that HMSO have no choice in this but it does seem a shame to spend all this money on websites and search engines to publish all this legislation for it to be of little use to the public or the profession.

Secondary
Scottish Statutory Instruments (S.S.I.s) are to be found on the HMSO site (**http://www.hmso.gov.uk**): follow the Scottish links to find them. They will be published on site as they become available.

Case Law

Scottish Courts
The Scottish Courts site (**http://www.scotcourts.gov.uk**) publishes court opinions of the Supreme and Sheriff Courts; Court of Session opinions from September 1998 and in commercial cases from January 1998 and criminal opinions from September 1998 of the High Court of Judiciary, including some sentencing appeals. Sheriff Court cases published on the site are those reported since September 1998 where there is a significant point of law or particular public interest. There

are two search methods: either by text or a structured search. The structured search is a search by judgment, type, date, party and type of action.

W. Green
The Scottish Law publishers W. Green's site (**http://www. wgreen.co.uk**) advertises the publication of the Scots Law Times on CD-ROM but does not provide accessible case reports on site. Several of the links were out of date when I visited.

Institutions

Scottish Parliament
The Scottish Parliament (**http://www.scottish.parliament.uk/**) has a very accessible site. There is information about the Scottish Parliament including lists of parliamentary questions, details of parliamentary business and an explanation of parliamentary procedure. There is also a very detailed list of all Bills currently before Parliament. The full text of Bills and policy memoranda are available to download in pdf. See p. 58 for details of where the necessary software can be downloaded.

Scottish Executive
The Scottish Executive (**http://www.scotland.gov.uk**) has a consumer friendly site with links to news and publications as well as to all the government departments where relevant papers and policy statements can be found.

Scottish Courts
The Scottish Courts site (**http://www.scotcourts.gov.uk**) publishes case reports and detailed information on the courts and court structure.

Law Society of Scotland
The Law Society of Scotland site (**http://www.lawscot.org.uk**) contains topical legal news and information on Scottish law as well as a complete list of solicitors and firms in Scotland.

Scottish Law Firms
Like the rest of the U.K., the majority of reasonably large Scottish law firms have web sites. The quality of these web sites, like the rest of

the U.K., is of varying quality. MacRoberts site (**http://www.
macroberts.co.uk**), mentioned above because of its international
links, is a good straightforward site with interesting legal news and
publications. A specialist criminal defence firm based in Glasgow
called Graham Walker (**http://www.webzone7.com/criminal-law/
about.htm**) has a small effective web site giving contact details and a
clear guide explaining what to do if you are arrested. There is also
"The Facts: A Guide to Drugs", maybe giving a clue as to the charges
laid against a lot of Graham Walkers' clients.

Other Scottish Sites

Society for Computers and Law
If you choose the local links button on The Society for Computers and
Law (**http://www.scl.org/welcome.htm**) and choose Scotland you will
find a good collection of Scottish links to Scottish legal web sites,
firms, professional associations and others.

Wales

Given the recent and only partial devolution there is not much of
purely Welsh law on the Internet but two sites that are worth
mentioning are listed below.

Legislation

Wales statutory instruments and draft Wales statutory instruments
from 1999 are published on the HMSO site (**http://hmso.gov.uk**):
follow the links to Wales.

National Assembly of Wales

The National Assembly has a clear easily accessible web site (**http://
www.wales.gov.uk/index.e.html**) including: Who's Who in the Welsh
Assembly, how it works, policy and information, Welsh legislation and
press releases. Following the Welsh legislation link gives access to
quite a depth of information on areas of interest to the Welsh
Assembly.

Northern Ireland

There is not much of purely Northern Irish law to find on the Internet. The Bailii Project is a start and in time there might even be some Northern Irish legislation as well.

British and Irish Legal Information Institute

The Bailii Project (**http://www.bailii.org**) site currently has the following case law:

- Northern Irish Court of Appeal decisions.
- Northern Irish High Court decisions.

Search facilities are available on site.

Republic of Ireland

The Republic of Ireland is quite well served by the Internet. All the major institutions of government are online as well as Irish statutes published between 1922 and 1997 and the full text of the Constitution. There is also development of purely Irish portals.

One area where there is very little free online, at present, is Irish case law though there are good subscription services available.

The British and Irish Legal Information Institute

The Bailii Project (**http://www.bailii.org**) includes the Irish legal system. Giving the possibility of free access to the law of all the major jurisdictions of these islands. At the present time the case law on the Irish site is quite limited with just a few Irish Supreme Court cases and about 50 Irish High Court decisions. But the Irish site does have the full text of all Irish statutes. There are still some teething troubles to be resolved with the presentation of the statutes and hyperlinking has not yet been added but it is a good start. Search facilities are available on site.

The Constitution

The Irish Constitution is available online from the Government of Ireland site (**http://www.irl.gov.ie**) together with basic information on the Irish government. Click on Houses of Oireachtas (Houses of Parliament) to link to the full text of the Irish Constitution.

Legislation

Irish legislation is published on the Internet by the Attorney General's Office (**http://www.irl.gov.ie/ag/**). Acts of the Oireachtas (Acts of Parliament) from 1922 to 1997 are currently available. The web site is slow. I am told this will be improved with the coming online of the updated Acts from 1922–98 together with statutory instruments and chronological tables. The statutes can also be bought in CD-ROM format. The statutes are fully searchable.

Case Law

There are, as yet, no free Irish case law services except the limited cases available on the Bailii Project site detailed above. Subscription services are available, notably Lexis-Nexis (**http://www.lexis-nexis.co.uk**).

Lexis-Nexis reports cases from the Irish Reports; Irish Law Reports Monthly; Irish Law Times and Judgments of the Court of Criminal Appeal.

FirstLaw (**http://www.firstlaw.ie**) publishes Irish case law but currently only on CD-ROM and quite a limited selection of cases dating from 1998.

Institutions

The Court Service site (**http://www.courts.ie**) provides information about the working of all the different courts with up to date information on legal issues relating to the Court Service.

The Law Society of Ireland has an informative site (**http://www.lawsociety.ie**) including the latest legal news and a long list of current legal vacancies as well as a useful list of all Acts passed in the preceding year.

The Bar Council of Ireland site (**http://www.indigo.ie/~gregk/**) contains information about the Bar and how to become a barrister. It also has links to other legal resources.

Firms and Barristers

Barristers in Ireland do not practice from Chambers, as a consequence there are very few bar web sites. The situation for solicitors on the other hand is very similar to the U.K. The majority of the larger firms have web sites, some are excellent with a lot of useful information. William Fry (**http://www.williamfry.ie**) and McCann-Fitzgerald (**http://www.mccann-fitzgerald.ie**) have interesting sites with news and legal briefings on current legal issues.

Other Irish Sites

Irish Law Links (**http://www.ucc.ie/depts/law/irishlaw**) is exactly what you would think it is: a set of links to all sites legal and Irish. There are links to the Irish Constitution, the legal systems of Ireland and Northern Ireland, the peace process and a host of others. There is also a discussion group for Irish lawyers.

FindLaw, the American law portal (**http://www.findlaw.com**) has some Irish law links though not that easy to find. On FindLaw's homepage you need to find the button for foreign and international countries, from there go to individual country pages. This will take you to a list from which you can choose Ireland.

Legal-Island is an Irish Portal (**http://www.legal-island.com**) with links to firms both North and South of the border as well as to legislation sites and other Irish legal sites.

Lawlinks (**http://www.lawlinks.ie**) is an Irish company that provides Internet services to Irish lawyers. Lawlinks is a subscription service providing access to Companies House, the Land Registry, personal and company judgments and company formations.

United States of America

Most corporate lawyers will at some time need to know about the U.S. legal system including federal and state law. The United States is a very large country with a complex legal system, but it is also where the Internet was developed. As a consequence, access to U.S. law on the Internet is pretty comprehensive. All of the U.S. codes are available from a number of sites as well as a large body of State and Federal case law. As there is so much U.S. law on the Internet and given that it is a foreign jurisdiction the easiest way to find your way around is through one of the legal portals. I have set out below a selection of U.S. portals of these FindLaw is probably the best known. I find it quite manageable and a useful resource. I have also added some U.S. government sites. These can be a useful place to look for law and for detailed research. In the section on other useful sites of particular interest is the Legal Information Institute site at Cornell, this hosts a very searchable edition of the U.S. codes.

U.S. Portals

FindLaw
FindLaw (**http://findlaw.com**) is probably the best known of the U.S. legal portals. I find the format of the homepages very crowded and off-putting, but they must be doing something right as they seem to be continually growing and very popular. On FindLaw's site you will find links to the U.S. codes, to Supreme and Federal Court judgments as well as links to the laws of the various states. All Supreme Court cases since 1937 are searchable by citation, case name and full text with hypertext links within the cases to other cited cases. There is a legal subject index to find links to any legal subject you can think of as well as links to legal journals, newsgroups and law firms. In fact if it is legal you will probably find it somewhere on FindLaw. It is also possible to link directly to LawCrawler, a specialist legal search engine, if the answers can't be found through the FindLaw site then you can send LawCrawler off into cyberspace to see if it is out there.

A couple of FindLaw sub-sites are worth mentioning. First, the FindLaw site for legal professionals (**http://profs.findlaw.com**) has a large number of articles by legal professionals on a wide range of topical legal issues. Secondly, the Cyberspace Law Centre (**http://cyber.findlaw.com**) is an excellent site with a comprehensive and searchable legal index of cyber law. There is information on e-commerce, intellectual property, censorship and the law of privacy. In fact just about everything you might want to know about cyber law. It is now possible to customize your FindLaw site, with My FindLaw, to give you quicker and easier access to the law you want (**http://login.findlaw.com/scripts/register**).

FindLaw also has mini portals to other jurisdictions. The U.K. portal is quite limited although FindLaw inform me that they are constantly improving the site.

Hieros Gamos
Hieros Gamos (**http://www.hg.org**) is very similar to FindLaw in content and uses FindLaw's database of caselaw. As you would expect there are links to the different branches of the U.S. government, to law journals, law firms and discussion groups. There are further links to international organisations, European sites and to 200 different legal topics.

Jurisline.com
Jurisline.com another U.S. legal portal (**http://jurisline.com**) is less cluttered on first impressions than FindLaw and therefore a bit easier on the eye. It contains a fully searchable case law facility for all the Federal District and Circuit Courts and 37 of the 50 states as well as the U.S. and New York code. The site appears to be aimed at the professional male with the Dow Jones index, stock quotes and when I last visited there was a banner advert for "Girls"!

The Oyez Project at NorthWestern University
The Oyez Project (**http://www.oyez.nwu.edu**) is a multimedia database of Supreme Court opinions in the field of constitutional law. Or more simply if you want to hear the original recordings of judgments given by U.S. Supreme Court justices in the great constitutional cases that have shaped the United States, then you can hear them here.

Jurist
Jurist (**http://jurist.law.pitt.edu**) bills itself as The Law Professor's Network. It contains legal news, searchable case law and legislation and access to the very latest decisions. A large number of legal articles are also accessible from the site.

Catalaw
Catalaw (**http://www.catalaw.com**) sells itself as a Meta-index of law and government and "the catalog of catalogs". The homepage for catalaw consists of three drop-down menus. You choose a legal topic, region and specify an "extra info page". These pages are to help you narrow down your search to a specific area. When you have chosen your categories Catalaw searches its links for you. It is quite straightforward to use but doesn't seem to throw up as much as FindLaw.

U.S. Government Sites

U.S. House of Representatives
The U.S. House of Representatives (**http://www.house.gov/**) site has a lot of material on the House and its members as well as links to a free, fully searchable and downloadable text of the U.S. codes organised by subject (**http://uscode.house.goc/usc.htm**).

Thomas

The Thomas site (**http://thomas.loc.gov**) is named after Thomas Jefferson. It provides U.S. legislative information on the Internet. It is possible to search Bills going through Congress by topic, Bill number or title. It is also possible to search for committee reports and to find out a lot of information about Congress.

The Senate

The Senate site (**http://www.senate.gov**) is quite limited in its ambition. It is possible to track Bills through the Senate but otherwise it is a matter of basic information about the Senate and its procedures. A useful resource (if you are an American) is the contact details for your Senator. If you are interested in art you can view specific pieces of the Senate art collection online.

Other Useful U.S. Sites

Legal Information Institute at Cornell University

The Legal Information Institute hosts a site for browsing the U.S. codes (**http://www.4.law.cornell.edu/uscode**). The codes can be found on a lot of other sites and through FindLaw and Hieros Gamos but this site provides an excellent searching mechanism to make the huge content of the Codes more accessible. Searching for U.S. Federal law on milk pasteurisation took two minutes!

Legal Journals on the Web

The legal journals site (**http://www.usc.edu/dept/law-lib/legal/journ als.html**) is a really good, easy to use site. The site essentially lists and links to a large number of U.S. law reviews.

Finding Federal Information

Librarians at the University of California established the Finding Federal Law site (**http://www.library.ucsb.edu/universe/dedecker. html**). The site gives a clear guide to locating government information on the web with comprehensive links to federal information. The site has some good ideas for legal research on the web applicable to all lawyers.

Law.com

A good site if you want to keep up with legal news in the States is Law.com (**http://www.law.com**). Law.com provides a comprehensive legal news service as well as selling legal products and advertising legal vacancies. An interesting feature of Law.com, and no doubt the way of all online news magazines, is the ability to customize the content of your Law.com depending upon where you live or whether you are a legal professional or studying law. There are, of course, specifically targeted banner advertisements depending upon where you are on the legal ladder.

Being the USA, there are also a lot of quirky (some more on the weird side) legal sites around. One I found captivating was the Smoking Gun site (**http://www.thesmokinggun.com**). If you want to see a copy of the Unabombers psychiatric report, the FBI files on Frank Sinatra and Dean Martin or Tom Cruises confidentiality clause this is the site for you. The site is, in a way, a testament to freedom of information in the States, all documents on the site coming from original government or law enforcement sources.

"Big Government. Small Brains. Dumb Laws." is the billing for another fun U.S. site. The Dumblaws site (**http://www.dumblaws.com**) has a breakdown of dumb laws by U.S. State and other countries. Did you know that the head of every household in Kennesaw, Georgia must possess a firearm? Or rather less worrying did you realise that it is illegal to keep a donkey in a bathtub in Georgia or to tie a giraffe to a telephone pole in Atlanta, GA?

Specialist Areas

The aim of this section is twofold. First, to provide a set of links in some of the core areas of legal practice. Secondly, and more importantly, to explain how to compile your own set of links on any area.

The process of compiling a set of links is a simple but time consuming task. If you follow the simple instructions below a library of web sites particularly suited to your legal interests can be created. In the lists below I have tried to balance the links available between government bodies, academic institutions, organisations, journals, firms, chambers and enthusiasts. Obviously if you were creating your own list it would be possible to focus in on the type of site that is of particular interest to you. But remember to be aware that the legal information on any given site might not be accurate or up to date, follow the tests on p. 38 to verify the quality of legal information.

To create your own list turn to the section in the book on portals on p. 137. Firstly select three or four different portals. With each portal go to the section on legal topics and search your topic of choice. Remember to bookmark each web site of interest. On an interesting site follow any links available to you, to see if there are more interesting sites to link to. When you come to the end of a trail use the back button on your browser to return to the portal and try another link. As a secondary source of web sites it is worth checking out the sites of the top solicitors and barristers in the field to see if there are any interesting publications or newsletters on site. The easiest way to do this is to use the Legal 500. This can be found at the International Centre for Commercial Law (**http://www. icclaw.com**). If you select the relevant work area follow the links to get the web address of the firm or chambers. Once you have worked through this process on a few portals and a selection of firms and chambers you should have built up a comprehensive and very useful set of web sites on your bookmark.

Business, Financial and Commercial

Business law is very well served on the web. There are a large number of free and subscription sites. An essential site for a lot of company lawyers would be the Companies House site. There are also excellent company news and briefing sites like Dow Jones Interactive and Bloombergs. The Westlaw subscription legal research site is heavily biased towards company and commercial lawyers with a lot of business information as well as regular law on site and as an all-in-one package it probably cannot be beaten in this area for content.

- Companies House **(http://www.companies-house.gov.uk)**

  Company searches, information, online filing and news.

- Companies Court **(http://www.courtservice.gov.uk)**

  Judgments, practice directions and notices.

- Financial Services Authority **(http://www.fsa.gov.uk)**

  Publications on site available for downloading in pdf.

- The London Stock Exchange **(http://londonstockex.co.uk)**

- The Bank of England **(http://www.bankofengland.co.uk)**

- The New York Stock Exchange **(http://www.nyse.com)**

- Lexis-Nexis **(http://www.lexis-nexis.co.uk)**

  Subscription only legal and business information service with extensive and searchable databases.

- Westlaw **(http://www.westlaw.co.uk)**

  Subscription only legal and business information service with extensive and searchable databases.

- Reuters Business Briefing **(http://www.bizinfo.reuters.com)**

- Dow Jones Interactive **(http://www.djinteractive.com)**

  Subscription service providing news and newswires from all over the world on companies, industries, countries and the financial markets.

- Mondaq Business Briefing **(http://www.businessmonitor.co.uk)**

  Site monitoring legislative and regulatory framework affecting business all over the world. Can browse site by topic or search for specific information.

- Law Money **(http://www.lawmoney.com)**

  Legal and business news site. Billed as the site for international legal counsel. Need to register for access to certain parts of site. Also access to the e-journals: Internet Law Review, Managing Intellectual Property and International Finance Law.

- Hemscott Legal **(http://www.hemscottlegal.com)**

  Legal and financial news including a disputes database detailing who acted for who and a Mergers and Acquisitions table, who merged, who acted as advisors, etc., and a lot more.

- Bloombergs **(http://www.bloomberg.com)**

  Specialists in financial information.

- Carol Online **(http://www.carol.co.uk)**

  Free online service offering access to companies' annual reports with searchable databases.

- Norton Rose **(http://www.nortonrose.com)**

  Like a lot of city firms Norton Rose publish articles on their web site which they think will be of interest to their clients. It is necessary to register on site to gain access, but access is free. There are a lot of publications on subjects from aviation to insurance law.

- Freshfields **(http://www.freshfields.com)**

  Freshfields have a dedicated sub-site for their competition and trade practices. A lot of articles on competition law, some in pdf, see p. 58. The latest two editions of Freshfields newsletters, competition comment and forecast (business law developments in the E.U.) are available online.

- Financial Services Internet Directory (**http://www.find.co.uk**)

  Extensive links to financial services sites.

- Business Information Services on the Internet (**http://www. dis.strath.ac.uk/business/index.html**)

  Links to business information on the Internet.

- UK Bankruptcy and Insolvency web site (**http://www.insolvency. co.uk**)

  Bankruptcy and insolvency law and information, insolvency practitioners and a searchable database of businesses in liquidation. Lists of businesses and assets for sale by receivers and administrators.

- European Company Lawyer's Association (**http://www.ecla.org**)

Constitutional and Administrative

Constitutional and administrative law is not very well served on the web. The parliament site is an exception to this general rule providing mountains of information on parliament and her proceedings. Otherwise in the field of Human Rights law the Crown Office Row site is worth visiting for a clear explanation of the Human Rights Act 1988.

- The Houses of Parliament (**http://www.parliament.uk**)

- Home Office publications and information on the Internet (**http:// www.homeoffice.gov.uk/pubs.htm**)

  Section of Home Office reports on constitutional and electoral matters.

- The Constitution Unit (**http://www.ucl.ac.uk/constitution-unit/ index.htm**)

  The Constitution Unit at University College London School of Public Policy is an independent research body on constitutional change. General information on site and you can download a publication called The Monitor. This is in pdf, see p. 58. The Monitor contains updates and commentary on latest developments in the governments constitutional reform program.

- The U.K. legal system on the Internet (**http://www.leeds.ac.uk/ law/hamlyn/intro.htm**)

  A product of Leeds University, this web site is a simple explanation of the fundamentals of the U.K. legal system.

- Magna Carta (**http://www.bl.uk**)

  The British Library web site has a lot of documents accessible online. To find the full translation of the Magna Carta search the site for "Magna Carta".

- One Crown Office Row (**http://www.enstarsw.co.uk/1cor_new/ indexanimated.asp**)

  Chambers site and home of human rights update. Full text of Human Rights Act 1998 and commentary.

- Researching constitutional law on the Internet (**http://www. lib.uchicago.edu/~llou/conlaw.html**)

  U.S. based site with extensive links to worldwide constitutional law.

- International constitutional law (**http://www.uni-wuerzburg.de/law/ index.html**)

  Information on hundreds of countries and their constitutions.

Criminal Law and the Criminal Justice System

There are quite a few interesting sites in the field of criminal law. The Court of Appeal judgments at the Court Service site are useful as are the Home Office publications and information available on their Internet site. This site is packed with information on criminal justice issues. One other site I found interesting was the set of links called JusticeLink on the King's College site.

- Court of Appeal and Crown Courts (**http://www.courtservice. gov.uk**)

  Judgments of Court of Appeal (Criminal Division) and Practice Directions and Notices for Court of Appeal and Crown Court.

- Crown Prosecution Service (**http://www.cps.gov.uk**)

  Publications on site include code for crown prosecutors.

- Legal Services Commission (**http://www.legalservices.gov.uk**)

  Information on the community legal service and the proposed criminal defence service.

- Community Legal Service (**http://www.justask.org.uk**)

  Very much a consumer orientated site with answers to basic questions.

- Magistrates Association (**http://www.magistrates-association. org.uk**)

- Magistrates Court Service (**http://www.open.gov.uk/lcd/magist/ magistfr.htm**)

  Lord Chancellor's Department site on Magistrates Courts includes links to reports on magistrates plus an explanation of the work of magistrates, legislation affecting and information on the appointment of magistrates.

- Serious Fraud Office (**http://www.sfo.gov.uk**)

  Published lectures on site on fraud.

- National Criminal Intelligence Service (**www.ncis.co.uk**)

- Criminal Cases Review Commission (**http://www.ccrc.gov.uk**)

- Home Office publications and information available on the Internet (**http://www.homeoffice.gov.uk/pubs.htm**)

  A huge quantity of government reports on criminal justice issues and links to Home Office Bills before parliament and the British Crime Survey.

- Home Office Research, Development and Statistics Directorate (**http://www.homeoffice.gov.uk/rds**)

  Statistical research and reports on criminal justice issues, some reports available online.

- The Stephen Lawrence enquiry (**http://www.homeoffice.gov.uk/ ppd/oppu/slawr.htm**)

- The MacPherson Report (**http://www.official-documents.co.uk/ document/CM42/4262/4262.htm**)

- The Criminal Justice system (**http://www.criminal-justice-system. gov.uk**)

  Links to all the major criminal justice agencies and some government reports on crime.

- Criminal Courts Review (**http://www.criminal-courts-review .org.uk**)

  Lord Justice Auld's review of the workings of the criminal justice system.

- Crime Online (**http://www.butterworths.co.uk**)

  Butterworths subscription service for criminal lawyers. It includes access to the All England reports, criminal law statutes and statutory instruments.

- King's College London Centre for Crime and Justice Studies (**http://www.kcl.ac.uk/depsta/rel/ccjs**)

  Includes Justicelink: a well thought out set of links on criminal justice issues.

- British Journal Of Criminology (**http://www.3oup.co.uk/crim/contents**)

  Well respected law journal available online to subscribers at approximately £40 per annum.

- Criminal Law Week (**http://www.criminal-law-week.co.uk**)

  Weekly digest of new developments in criminal law available online to subscribers at approximately £135 per annum.

Employment

There are a large number of sites for employment lawyers on the Internet. Sites of interest include the Employment Appeals Tribunal site and Thompsons Labour and European Law Review. This is a free monthly online journal on the law as it effects trade unions and their members. For more discussion of employment law issues the incomes data services site is interesting.

- Employment Appeals Tribunal (**http://www.employmentappeals.gov.uk**)

  Judgments and information on the working of the court.

- Department of Trade and Industry (**http://www.dti.gov.uk**)

  Information for employers and employees.

- Commission for Racial Equality (**http://www.cre.gov.uk**)

  Individuals rights and the law on discrimination with commentary on relevant statutes.

- Trade Union Congress (**http://www.tuc.org.uk**)

  In biz ed for students section straightforward explanation of employment law.

- Advisory, Conciliation and Arbitration Services (ACAS) (**http://www.modus.co.uk/clients/acas**)

- British Employment law (**http://www.emplaw.co.uk**)

  Subscription service for employment lawyers.

- Employment Law Service (**http://www.cchnewlaw.co.uk**)

  Subscription service for employment lawyers including case databases, updating and fortnightly journal.

- Lawrite (**http://www.lawrite.co.uk**)

  Site selling employment law CD-ROM.

- Incomes Data Services (**http://www.incomesdata.co.uk**)

  Useful articles and comment on topical employment law issues and employment law cases.

- Thompsons Labour and European Law Review (**http://www. thompsons.law.co.uk/text/libindex.htm**)

  Free monthly online journal on U.K. and European law affecting trade unions and members from Thompsons the trade union solicitors. Extensive number of detailed articles on broad range of employment law issues. Need pdf to download, see p. 58 but you can view online.

- Barrister Daniel Barnett (**http://www.danielbarnett.co.uk**)

  Barrister's site with employment law articles. Also possible to subscribe to employment law list on site or by sending blank e-mail to: employment_law_UK-subscribe@listbot.com.

Family

All the different arms of government that are involved in the family can be found on the Internet and not surprisingly that is also where you will find quite a lot of the information that family lawyers are looking for.

The Lord Chancellor's Department site is a must for all family lawyers. Otherwise I imagine that the Child Support Agency and the civil procedure rules sites might be on a lot of bookmarks.

- Lord Chancellor's Department (**http://www.open.gov/lcd/family/ famfr.htm**)

This site contains Consultation Papers, the Family Law Act 1997 and links to the Ancillary Relief Pilot Scheme.

- Civil procedure rules (**http://www.open.gov./lcd** and **http://www. beagle.org.uk/cpr**)

- Legal services commission (**http://www.legalservices.gov.uk**)

  Legal aid information.

- Court Service Family Division (**http://www.courtservice.gov.uk**)

  Only one case was online from the family division at the time of writing. Family division practice directions and notices can also be found on site.

- Official Solicitor's Department (**http://www.offsol.demon.co.uk**)

  Information on wardship, adoption and child abduction.

  Explanation of legal basis of official solicitor including statutory authority and rules of court.

- The Social Security and Child Support Commissioners Decisions (**http://www.hywels.demon.co.uk/commrs/decns.htm**)

- Child Support Agency (**http://www.dss.gov.uk/csa**)

- Solicitor's Family Law Association (**http://www.sfla.org.uk**)

- Law Society (**http://www.lawsociety.co.uk**)

  Choose law society members and then family. Several articles on family law.

- The International Journal of Law, Policy and the Family (**http:// www.3oup.co.uk/lawfam**)

  An online legal journal from Oxford University Press, subscriptions approximately £85 per annum.

- National Family Mediation Service (**http://www.nfm.u-net.com**)

  Family law and mediation information.

- International Academy of Matrimonial Lawyers (**http://www.iaml. org**)

  A U.S. based organisation.

- Jordan's Family Law (**http://www.familylaw.co.uk**)

  Family law update—online summaries of the latest cases, legislation and practice developments.

- The Family Law Consortium (**http://www.tflc.co.uk**)

Updates on changes in the law and advice for clients on family law topics.

- Pannone and Partners (**http://www.pannone.co.uk**)

  Straightforward articles on family law aimed at the public.

- Pearl Willis's Law site (**http://www.zyworld.com/familylaw**)

  Barristers web page. A lot of information on family law issues, case summaries and family law links.

- Terry Lynch's Law site (**http://www.terrylynch.co.uk/Family% 20Law.htm**)

  Barrister's web page. Papers on topical family law issues.

- One Mitre Court Buildings (**http://www.1mcb.com**)

  Specialist family law set. Recent cases and developments in family law, grossing-up calculator, income tax rates and bands.

- Families Need Fathers (**http://www.fnf.org.uk**)

  Packed with family law, information and links. Topics include changing a child's surname, family mediation and papers on fatherhood and parenting.

- Child Rights Information Network (**http://www.crin.org**)

- Family Discussion List: **law-family@mailbase.ac.uk**.

  To subscribe e-mail: law-family-request@mailbase.ac.uk.

- The Couples Place (**http://www.couples-place.com**)

  "Your online learning community for solving marriage problems", including communal storytelling and "Everyday Love" a Valentines Workshop for couples.

Intellectual Property

Not surprisingly, given the involvement of I.P. law and lawyers in the Internet, the quality and quantity of sites relevant to intellectual property law surpasses most other areas.

There are a lot of very good sites including the Patent Agency site packed with information on patents and patent law. Also definitely worth a look is the Intellectual Property Rights Helpdesk. This is an E.U. site again full of information and links.

- Patent Office (**http://www.patent.gov.uk**)

Patent, trademark and copyright information, searchable databases and judgments.

- Patent Court (**http://www.courtservice.gov.uk**)

  Selection of patent court decisions, practice directions and notices.

- Data Protection Registrar (**http://www.open.gov.uk/dpr/dprhome. htm**)

  Lots of advice and guidance on data protection issues.

- Copyright Licensing Agency (**http://www.cla.co.uk**)

- Chartered Institute of Patent Agents (**http://www.dircon.co.uk/ cipa**)

- European Patent Office (**http://www.european-patent-office.org**)

  Information on how to register a European patent.

- U.S. Patent and Trade Mark Office (**http://www.uspto.gov**)

- World Intellectual Property Organisation (**http://www.wipo.org**)

- E-Pages: International Journal of Law and Information Technology (**http://www.3oup.co.uk/inttec**)

  Online legal journal from Oxford University Press, subscriptions start at £50 per annum.

- I.P. Magazine (**http://www.ipmag.com**)

  U.S. online intellectual property magazine for lawyers.

- Intellectual Property Rights Helpdesk (**www.cordis.lu/pr-help desk/en/home.html**)

  An impressive intellectual property law resource. An E.U. site containing comprehensive information on patents trademarks and copyrights for all E.U. countries. Links to national patent offices and search facilities through **esp@cenet**. It is possible to subscribe on site for a free monthly newswire on I.P. issues.

- Oxford Intellectual Property Research Centre (**http://www. oiprc.ac.uk**)

  Academic research centre, papers online in pdf (see p. 58) on numerous I.P. topics.

- Script (**http://www.law.ed.ac.uk/script/pubs.htm**)

  Script is the centre for research in intellectual property and technology at the University of Edinburgh. Limited online publications but really extensive I.P. links.

- Researching International Intellectual Property Law: Internet Resources by Lyonette Louis-Jaques (**http://lib.uchicago.edu/ ~llou/intlip.html**)

  An extensive list of intellectual property links with a U.S. bias.

- Jenkins Chartered Patent Agents (**http://www.jenkins-ip.com**)

  Extensive intellectual property information and U.K. I.P. statutes and commentary.

- Bird and Bird (**http://www.twobirds.com**)

  Top I.P. firm lots of information on site on brands, trademarks and general I.P.

- Bristows (**http://www.bristows.com**)

  Another top I.P. firm again with a lot of I.P. publications on site including updates in different areas of I.P. Law.

- European Intellectual Property Law List (**http://www.ipjur.com/ html/intprop.htm**)

  Keep up to date on current I.P. issues by subscribing to I.P. law list.

Personal Injury and Medical Negligence

For some reason there are a lot of subscription sites aimed purely at personal injury lawyers. The College of Law has set up a Personal Injury Virtual College in conjunction with the Association of Personal Injury Lawyers. This site is worth a look and may be a slice of things to come. It would also be useful for most personal injury lawyers to bookmark one of the medical sites as they can quickly check out any new medical terminology or condition. I have put one in the list, there are a lot of others.

- Court of Appeal (Civil Division) (**http://www.courtservice.gov.uk**)
- Civil Procedure Rules (**http://ww.open.gov.uk/lcd** or **http://www. beagle.org.uk/cpr**)
- Supreme Court Fee Order (**http://www.courtservice.gov.uk/ scfees.htm**)
- County Court Fee Order (**http://www.courtservice.gov.uk/ ccfees.htm**)
- Law Commission (**http://www.lawcom.gov.uk/library/lib-com.htm**)

Law commission reports on personal injury and damages.

- Association of Personal Injury Lawyers (**http://www.apil.com**)
- College of Personal Injury Lawyers (**http://www.cpil.net**)

Personal Injury Virtual College established by APIL and the College of Law details of courses and qualifications on site.

- Forum of Insurance Lawyers (**www.foil.org.uk**)

Foil is trying to do for the defendant's insurance market what APIL has done for the plaintiff market.

- Headway—National Head Injuries Association (**http://www.head way.org**)
- Civil Justice Council (**http://www.open.gov.uk.civjustice**)
- Law Society (**http://www.lawsociety.co.uk**)

Click on Law Society members and then the button for personal injury and/or civil litigation to find articles, news and consultation papers relevant to these areas of law.

- P.I. Online (**http://www.butterworths.co.uk**)

Butterworths' subscription service for personal injury lawyers, cases, legislation and updating.

- Current Legal Information (**http://www.smlawpub.co.uk**)

A Sweet and Maxwell subscription service, particularly useful for P.I. lawyers because of the extensive database of quantum cases.

- Lawtel (**http://www.interactive-lawyer.com**)

Subscription service from Lawtel, P.I. specialist area and quantum reports.

- Medical Litigation Online (**http://www.medneg.com**)

Subscription service for medical negligence practitioners including cases, articles and new developments.

- Exchange Chambers (**http://www.exchangechambers.co.uk**)

Liverpool set with P.I. newsletter on site including commentary on P.I. developments and summary of recent cases.

- New Baily Chambers (**http://www.newbaily.co.uk**)

P.I. links and pain, suffering and loss of amenity calculator to assist P.I. practitioners in applying the decision in *Heil* v. *Rankin*.

- Patient UK (**http://www.patient.co.uk**)

  U.K. medical links and directory to help non-medical people to find information on health and health issues.

Property

There are a lot of property law sites that every property lawyer should have bookmarked. The first is obviously the land registry. With the possibilities of online title transfers and more on the horizon, the land registry will be playing a pivotal role.

Other sites worth thinking about bookmarking are the Hardwicke Building site for keeping up to date in property law and the Law Society Gazette for their property law reports.

- The Land Registry (**http://www.landreg.gov.uk**)
- The High Court (**http://www.courtservice.gov.uk**)

  Judgments and practice directions.

- Ordinance Survey (**http://www.ordsvy.gov.uk**)

  A useful resource. It is possible to buy O.S. maps online.

- Estates Gazette Interactive (**http://www.propertylaw.co.uk**)

  Property law subscription service includes a complete archive of cases from Estates Gazette as well as detailed legal information on all aspects of property law.

- International Centre for Commercial Law (**http://www.icclaw.com**)

  U.K. commercial property law articles produced in association with Simmons and Simmons. Follow links from legal zones to commercial property.

- Leasehold Advisory Service (**http://www.lease-advice.org**)

  Publications on leasehold law on site and leasehold valuation tribunal decisions under Leasehold Reform Act 1993 and Landlord and Tenant Acts 1985 and 1987.

- Denton Wilde Sapte (**http://www.dentonhall.com**)

  A long list of property articles available for reading on site and for downloading in pdf, see p. 58.

- Hardwicke Building Property Group (**http://www.hardwicke.co.uk**)

An impressive chambers site. The property group section contains news, articles and summaries of recent important cases. A good site for keeping up to date with new developments.

- Falcon Chambers (**http://www.falcon-chambers.com**)

The specialist property set. A selection of property law articles on site.

- Gary Webber's Property Law for Solicitors and Surveyors (**http://www.garywebber.co.uk**)

An impressive site from barrister and author Gary Webber includes lengthy articles on property law and the civil procedure rules and on boundary disputes as well as property news and notices.

- Landlord and Tenant News (**http://www.btinternet.com/~david.b.taylor/index.htm**)

A site from barrister David Taylor on landlord and tenant law with summaries of cases, articles and commentaries.

- Roger Horne's Miscellany (**http://www.number7.demon.co.uk**)

Commentary and articles on property and land law and a lot of other musings.

- Law Society Gazette—Property Law Reports (**http://www.law gazette.co.uk**)

For latest property reports go to Gazette in Practice, for earlier reports search the archives.

Legal Journals

Most legal practices subscribe to at least a few law journals. The larger practices to a lot. All lawyers and law students need law journals: to keep up to date with new legal developments and as a research tool. The provision of legal journals is an area of obvious growth on the Internet. At the moment there are a few e-journals but hundreds of others with no Internet presence. As these journals almost certainly exist in electronic form prior to publication it appears to be only a matter of time before it is possible to purchase either a paper subscription or an electronic subscription to the journal of your choice. In this section I have set out ways to go about finding law journals on the web and given brief details of some of the publications that are already online. Of all the sites mentioned the Ingenta site could prove to be very useful. The simplicity of the Oxford University Press site and services is also impressive.

In the States there are a lot of e-journals. This is partly because the penetration of the Internet is greater in the States but also because of the different culture in legal education. In the States nearly all law schools publish a law review, some of very high quality. These law reviews are usually free because they are published by a university rather than a publisher and are online almost automatically because it would seem strange not to put them online. The universities in the States have been at the forefront of pushing the Internet forward not only in technology but also in different applications for that technology.

Finding Law Journals

Electronic Law Journals

The University of Warwick maintains a useful site called the Electronic Law Journals Environment (**http://www.elj.warwick.ac.uk/**). This site established in 1997 was designed to help law students, academics and practitioners find information about U.K. law journals. To access follow the link on the homepage to "about law journals". The site contains a list of U.K. law journals that can be browsed by title or a search can be made for words included in the title of a journal. Information is provided on the current electronic status of the journal, is it fully online or are abstracts provided? If there is an Internet presence links are provided, if not, links are provided to the publishers web site. In addition for all journals, the publishers details, the journals ISSN number and the price and frequency of publication are available.

One note of caution, when I last visited some of the information had not been updated. In particular a journal that is fully online was listed as not being so. The pace of change is fast and it is not always possible to keep up.

Legal Journals on the Web

Legal Journals on the Web (**http://www.usc.edu/dept/law-lib/legal/journals.html**) is a U.S. site maintained by the University of Southern California. It is not only useful for finding U.S. journals but also has a section on foreign law journals and commercial law journals (which includes some U.K. publications). There is a very straightforward indexing system to explain exactly what is available online. Again, like the Electronic Law Journal site, when I last visited some of the information was out of date and some of the categorisation of journals was a bit weird, for example, the British Journal of Criminology can be found in amongst the commercial law journals. But this is still a useful site.

Ingenta

Ingenta (**http://www.ingenta.com**) bills itself as a global research gateway. It is a single point of free access to over 2,500 online journals. There are only 26 law journals on the system at the moment but this will increase. It is possible to view abstracts and the index of journals free. To view the full text of a journal it is necessary to be a subscriber to that publication. For academic institutions it is possible to obtain access to the whole database for a fee.

The Jurist

The Jurist site (**http://www.law.cam.ac.uk/jurist/index.htm**) has a selective list of law journals with some Internet presence.

Legal Portals

A good law portal should have links to sites where legal journals are listed or give information on specific e-journals. See LawLinks (**http://www.library.ukc.ac.uk/**) or Delia Venables (**http://www.venables.co.uk**). For U.S. journals try links from Findlaw (**http://www.findlaw.com**) or Hieros Gamos (**http://www.hg.org**).

Legal Publishers

If you are looking for a particular journal and you know the publisher it is always worth checking their web site for links to the journal or more information.

For instance you can link to the New Law Journal directly from Butterworth's web site (**http://www.butterworthsdirect.co.uk**). Another publishers' site worth checking out is the Oxford University Press (OUP) site (**http://www.oupjournals.org**). OUP have a wide ranging selection of online journals including The Oxford Journal of Legal Studies and The Statute Law Review. Current subscribers to any journal can access that journal online.

Not every legal publisher is taking the same route. For example, Sweet and Maxwell plan to make journals available online but only through WestLaw. Individual subscribers will have to buy the paper copy.

Specific E-Journals

New Law Journal

The New Law Journal (**http://www.butterworths.co.uk/nlj**) is a weekly journal published by Butterworths containing a broad range of articles on contemporary legal issues. It is available online to subscribers, prices start at £67 per annum for students, up to £170 for practitioners. It is possible to read the lead article each week free of charge and to view the index.

Web Journal of Current Legal Issues

The Web Journal of Current Legal Issues (**http://webjcli.ncl.ac.uk**) has been published online since 1995 and is a joint production of the University of Newcastle Law School and Blackstones. Issues covered include judicial decisions, law reform, legal research and technology and practice. The Web Journal is published twice a month and is free.

Journal of Information Law and Technology

The Journal of Information Law and Technology (**http://elj.warwick. ac.uk/jilt**) was the first U.K. e-journal, it is published three times per year by the CTI Law Technology Centre at the University of Warwick in conjunction with the Centre for Law, Technology and Computing at Strathclyde University. The journal contains a selection of refereed articles on issues relating to information technology and law and applications of information technology in law.

The ambition behind JILT was to establish a high standard for electronic law journals, to facilitate faster publication of law journals and to encourage debate. Hyperlinks are provided within the text of articles to primary and secondary sources. JILT is free and exists only in electronic form.

Thompsons Labour and European Law Review

Thompsons solicitors (**http://www.thompsons.law.co.uk/text/libindex .htm**) publish this free monthly online journal on employment law issues.

Criminal Law Week

Criminal Law Week (**http://www.criminal-law.co.uk**) is available on subscription at approximately £135 per annum. It contains digests of recent developments in criminal law.

CHAPTER TWO

LEGAL RESEARCH ONLINE

It has been argued that legal publishers are a dying breed as the services they offer will no longer be needed with the arrival of free legal information available over the Internet. I would disagree with this prognosis. Although legal publishers will no longer be able to sell to the legal community, statutes, statutory instruments and case law or "old rope" as Laurie West-Knights of Bailii so delicately put it. They can still offer a range of services not provided elsewhere like targeted updating and alerts, commentary, hyperlinking between databases and the speed of provision of new judgments online. The subscription services also come with a guarantee of accuracy and reliability not found at a lot of sites on the Internet. They should also be quick and easy to use. If the online legal publishers can keep on adding value to black letter law there will be a market for them. The real question is will a case or statute be published on paper at all in five years time?

Subscription Services

This section looks at the online subscription services provided to lawyers by the legal publishers. Focusing on the sites that offer law from a range of sources, services that are purely case law-based are reviewed in the case law section, see p. 47. All lawyers in practice and law students through their law school libraries need to be familiar with the different services provided and to decide (if they have a choice) which service is the most appropriate for their method of working and area and type of legal research.

There are four main providers: Sweet and Maxwell (Westlaw and Current Legal Information), Butterworths (Butterworths Direct and Lexis), Centaur (Lawtel and EU Interactive) and Context Ltd (Justis On-Line).

Each publisher provides a different service from the city biased all encompassing Westlaw to the case summaries and updating facilities available on Lawtel. It is impossible to say which is the best service overall as they have such different functions. But services that stand out for me are the Case and Legislation Locator documents from Westlaw, the provision of Halsbury's Laws online from Butterworths and the updating and case summaries from Lawtel and Lexis's database.

Most of the services can be understood with minimal instruction. But with the Westlaw service, training would be essential to ensure that all users understand how to use the different services provided. Without training on Westlaw it is likely that users would just skim over the surface and never really get to grips with the more complex functions.

For ease of use I have reviewed each site by breaking the information down into four sections: content, tools, searching and subscription.

Westlaw (http://westlaw.co.uk)

Westlaw is very well known in the states but still a bit of a newcomer in the U.K., part of the Thompson Group, Westlaw is being brought into the U.K. market by its sister company Sweet and Maxwell. WestlawUK was launched in Spring 2000 and at the time of writing was hot off the press. Like all these sites it is very much a work in progress and it will be interesting to see how it develops from its case law and commercially centred starting point.

Westlaw is a subscription only service and is not cheap. The company is aiming its product at large commercial firms so the prices and content are pitched accordingly.

The Westlaw site is huge but surprisingly manageable. The screens are simple with very few distracting graphics and follow a logical progression in all areas. Westlaw is not geared up for browsing. It is not possible to scan reports, journals or newspapers for relevant articles. The feel is that of a professional service, the plan seems to be to get in, do your search, charge your client and get out.

Content

Westlaw is too big to list all the contents. The following is a summary:

Case law materials include:

The Law Reports

Lloyd's Law Reports

Fleet Street Reports

Environmental Law Reports

Entertainment and Media Law Reports

European Patent Office Reports

Common Market Law Reports

United Kingdom Transcripts

Legislative materials include:

The Consolidated Law in Force covering company, commercial, intellectual property, property, tax, personal injury, rules of the supreme and county court. It is also possible to check legislation at a historic date from 1992 using the U.K. Law in Force Historic Database. The coverage for statutory instruments began in 1948.

Law reviews

A selection of U.K. and U.S. law reviews. It is intended in time that the content of all of Sweet and Maxwell's 60 law journals will be available through Westlaw.

Current Awareness Facilities

These are extensive and includes summaries of case transcripts, statutory instruments, progress of Bills through to the Royal Assent, Green Papers, White Papers, press releases and European Commission documents.

Business and Financial Information

Search facilities are available for all of the major papers and business journals together with Reuters and Dow Jones Interactive.

Tools

Locator Documents

The Locator Document or LocDoc in Westlaw speak is a document that tells you everything about a case or piece of legislation. The Case Locator Document includes a summary of the case, where the case has been reported, legislation and cases referred to and hypertext links to documents that are in the Westlaw database. The Legislation Locator Document gives commencement dates, in force dates together with links to enabling, delegated, referenced legislation, case law and journals. It is possible to check the state of an Act at a particular date post 1992. The Locator documents are a very straightforward way to research a case or Act and its development. In essence they are your research and updating all in one.

WestClip

WestClip is a news and legal development monitoring service. It can download, e-mail or print out documents and news stories on any subject specified. To use the service you need to enter search terms and the frequency you want WestClip to report. So, if you had a client involved in the Internet and offshore betting. You could set your search terms and get a weekly or daily report on new government proposals, regulations and news comment on the industry. If you used the service in conjunction with Chargeback you could bill your client for keeping you up to date with developments in their field.

UK Alert, Red Flag, Consolidation and Versioning

The U.K. Alert facility enables you to store information on an upcoming judgment so that when it is reported a transcript of the judgment is dispatched to a place of your choice.

Red Flag alerts a researcher if a case has been overturned, reversed or superceded.

Consolidation and Versioning enables you when researching to choose whether to see legislation as fully consolidated or prior to any amendments.

Chargeback

The Chargeback facility enables the cost of any research on Westlaw to be charged automatically to your clients' file.

Searching

It would be impossible to search across all the databases so I have focused on case law as these databases were more developed at the time of writing. As a general point I found the case law databases much easier to navigate than the legislation databases.

> I needed to find out whether the law on Article 177 references under the European Community Treaty in *Bulmer* v. *Bollinger* is still sound. I have the name of the case but I don't have a citation. In this situation finding the case is very simple. On the Welcome to Westlaw screen under Find a Case, fill in the 'Name' box and press Go. Seven cases come up, six of them from the Bulmer and Bollinger saga. The Case Locator document of the first case is on screen, it is simply a matter of scrolling through the Case Locator documents of the cases until I come to the relevant one. I find it at *H.P. Bulmer Ltd.* v. *J. Bollinger* S.A. (No. 2) 1974 Ch. 401. I can read the summary on screen, link to the full text of the case and return very simply to the Case Locator document. Cases where this case has been applied, considered or referred to are hyperlinked to give a really good overall picture of the current state of the law on Article 177 references. Legislation referred to in the case is listed but not hyperlinked, as the databases on European law have not been added to the system yet. I am told that European legislation will be up and running by July 2000.

Searches generally can be by natural language or using Boolean operators. There is good easily accessible information from the search screen to help you learn search techniques fast. To find legislation I found it easiest to use the field search by typing in the name of the Act or S.I. into the preliminary box and section number into the caption box. One criticism I would make is that it is not always clear why you cannot find something. Life would be easier if, when the information you were searching for was not on a database, you were told that was the reason you could not find it.

Subscription

Westlaw is initially aimed at the top commercial firms. It is therefore expensive. It is not sold on an individual subscription basis so it is difficult to assess exactly how much it does cost. Suffice to say those who have it can afford it.

Buy and use this service:

- If you can afford it.
- In commercially centred practices.
- To keep up to date in any area using WestClip.
- To thoroughly research and update using Locator documents.
- To make sure your client pays for the service with Chargeback.

Butterworths Direct (http://www.butterworths.co.uk)

Butterworths direct is a collection of different databases covering legislation, case law, updating and specialist sections. This makes it possible for a firm or chambers to select the databases to best suit their needs. Butterworths is not offering a seamless service broken down into individual databases. There are different search facilities on the sites and the databases are not fully hyperlinked. For instance, all references to All England Reports in Halsbury's Laws are hyperlinked while the reverse is not the case. That said these are early days with all these sites and it will be interesting to see how this one develops.

The screens in all the databases are set out on the same principle, a tree of chapters, statutes or cases on the left and text on the right. This makes the screen seem a little crowded but the downside is easily outweighed by the benefits of being able to browse, particularly in Halsbury's Laws. It is also possible to choose your screen layout to view text on the whole screen. There is also a different system of reading through material on screen, scrolling is available for reading each individual page, but to load the next page you need to click the page down button. This was a bit strange at first but very straightforward once you got used to it.

Content

Butterworths Direct as a whole is a very large site but because of the way it is presented it is broken down into digestible chunks. Some of the more specialist sections, such as P.I. and Crime Online are referred to in the specialist areas section, see pp. 97 and 104.

The content of the main databases is set out below.

- All England Direct.
- All England Law Reports 1936 to date.
- All England Reporter: latest developments and next day digests.
- Official Transcripts: October 1997 to date.
- Noter-up: check whether case reported in All England's or Official Transcript available.

The All England Law Reports are cross referenced to Halsbury's Laws, Halsbury's Statutes and Statutory Instruments but the only hyperlinks are to other All England cases referred to in a particular report. Where a case has been referred to in another case, there is a mark in the text to pinpoint the part of the text referred to. Potentially a very useful service was the "Additional Information" that was provided for some cases. Additional Information involved giving a list of cases where the case in question had been considered, distinguished or applied. It was not immediately clear why this additional information was given on some cases and not on others or whether it was going to be expanded to all cases.

Law Direct

The Law Direct database is sold as an updating service and essentially contains summaries of cases, acts and statutory instruments. Up dates can be received by e-mail if requested. Law Direct offers other services in addition to the case and legislation summaries including: information on the progress of legislation, a transcript ordering service, company searches, an articles citator and Is it in Force?

The Acts and statutory instrument databases offer narrative digests of Acts or statutory instruments issued since the beginning of 1995, this can be particularly useful with statutory instruments helping you to get to the meaning without having to wade through so much dry copy. There is also a case database giving summaries of cases since the beginning of 1995, no doubt this will be much in use by students. The civil procedure service on Law Direct gives the full amended text of the civil procedure rules and practice directions.

Halsbury's Laws

The big difference Butterworths has over other providers is Halsbury's Laws. It is still the only comprehensive narrative explanation of the law of England and Wales. Halsbury's Laws Direct is made up of the 50 volume set and the cumulative supplement and the monthly noters-up which are merged with the main text each month. So no more fumbling around trying to find the right volume and laboriously checking that the information is up to date. There are hyperlinks to All England Law Direct and to other parts of Halsbury's Laws but not to Legislation Direct. If any body of information was already formulated for Internet access this has to be it, the structure in volumes and the breakdown into chapters and sections lends itself very well to Internet research and browsing. It makes using the Internet version very like using the real thing but easier.

Legislation Direct

Legislation Direct contains the full amended text of U.K. statutes and statutory instruments as well as Scottish statutes and statutory instruments from 1998 onwards. Is it in Force? and a facility tracking the progress of legislation is also available. If there is new material that hasn't yet been incorporated into the database a red "Stop Press" sign appears. If you click on this sign, amendments, repeals and other recent developments will appear. Butterworths promise that the information is up to date within four to five working days. Statutes accurate at a particular historical point can be ordered by e-mail.

EU Direct Gold

EU Direct Gold offers European legal developments, access to legislation and cases via the Europa site and a dedicated enquiry bureau to enable subscribers to e-mail, fax or call for assistance. One useful feature on site is the database of directives and their corresponding U.K. legislation. You can find this under the U.K. implementation button.

Tools

Law Direct offers an e-mail update service where developments of your choice are e-mailed to you and there is the Stop Press facility for recent developments in Legislation Direct. Otherwise, Butterworths doesn't really get involved in providing fancy tools.

Searching

Suprisingly, there isn't a uniform search engine for Butterworths Direct. Each site has its own search facilities with slightly different terminology and different attributes. On the Halsbury's Laws site there is a natural language search facility called "Eureka!" while on legislation direct there is a choice of "Navigator" to locate a particular statute or a general search for more broad-based searching. A similar system to this exists in the All England Direct database. Whichever method used to search I found the searching quite straightforward, with good information and easily accessible search techniques.

I concentrated my searching on Halsbury's Laws though I did try searches in all the other main databases.

> I had a query regarding whether a church could refuse permission to a relative to put a photograph of the deceased on a grave site in a churchyard, just the sort of query Halsbury's Laws were made for. In any other database it would have been very difficult to know where to start. I did a natural language search looking for "Churchyards and gravestones and photographs". I was immediately directed to several sources of relevant law in the Ecclesiastical Volume and particularly to the case of *Re St. Mary's, Fawkham* [1981] 1 W.L.R. 1171 where it was stated that "photographs on tombstone inappropriate in an English country churchyard." I was able, very simply, to establish statutory authorities and case law to enable me to plan further research on the subject.

Buy and use this service:

- If you are a law student for Halsbury's Laws and Law Direct summaries.

- For the ability to select only the databases you need.
- For the All England Law Reports.

Subscription

Butterworths Direct price their products individually and per user.

Subscriptions for Halsbury's Laws start at £1950 per annum for a single user up to £4485 per annum for six to ten users. Civil Procedure Online starts at £350 per annum and All England Direct at £1520 per annum both for single users.

Lexis-Nexis (http://www.lexis-nexis.com)

When I was an articled clerk if you wanted to use Lexis you had to ask the librarian to conduct a search for you. There was one computer terminal that sat in the corner of the library guarded by the librarian. Lexis was too complicated and expensive for articled clerks. This shows just how long Lexis has been around giving it time to grow organically and to evolve from what was a unique but complex product into something much simpler. I have only looked at Lexis-Nexis Professional as this is the law based product from Lexis, there are other more business orientated products.

The navigation bar and search screens are simply set out and easy to use. The Help information is particularly good. While training on Lexis might make your initial searching easier it shouldn't take long to execute more complicated searches, so long as you read the information provided.

One aspect of Lexis I found surprising was the lack of hyperlinking between documents. For instance, neither cases nor statutes referred to in judgments are connected by hyperlinks. This seems a surprising omission given the length of time Lexis has been around.

Content

Lexis originated in the U.S. and if you look at the source directory you can see that there is a lot of U.S. legal information on the system. This information is available for searching as is legal information from numerous other jurisdictions, but it is possible to restrict your searches to the U.K.

Legal Research Online

The U.K. and E.U. databases contain the following:

Case law

Reported cases from 1936 for the All England Reports and Law Reports and Weekly Law Reports as well as specialist reports such as the Estates Gazette, Lloyd's Law Reports, Reports of Patent Cases, Simon's Tax cases and the Fleet Street Reports. Since 1980 unreported cases have been made available from among others the House of Lords, Privy Council, Court of Appeal (Civil Division) and the Queen's Bench Division. Scottish and Northern Ireland Case Reports are also available.

Primary U.K. legislation

Current Public and General Acts of England and Wales including Acts enacted but not yet in force from 1267 to the present. Local Acts are not included. The Acts are amended to include repeals and amending legislation.

Secondary U.K. legislation

Current statutory rules, regulations and orders of England and Wales from 1861 to the present day. Statutory instruments are amended by incorporating or removing relevant text.

E.U. Cases

Decisions of the Court of Justice and the Court of First Instance as contained in Celex (the legal database produced by the European Community).

E.U. Legislation

Treaties, international agreements, secondary legislation, supplementary legislation and parliamentary questions as contained in the Celex database.

Lexis contains a lot more information including a small but searchable selection of U.K. journals, news and other legal sources.

Tools

Lexis is quite a simple system providing a large database of information and some very refined search facilities. A couple of tools are worth mentioning. One is the ability to "Tag" documents. As you go through your search if you see a document that interests you, you can tag it. This effectively saves it to one side, then when you have finished your search you will be asked whether you want to download, e-mail or fax the tagged document.

Another tool is the "more like this" button. If you have conducted a search and found one document that particularly interests you, press the "more like this" button. A new list will come up with the search criteria taken from your original search and information from the selected document. It is also possible to select text out of a document to further refine your "more like this" search.

> I was looking at the *Hamilton* v. *Al Fayed* transcript from *The Times*, March 28, 2000. I pressed the "more like this" button and came up with a couple of other cases with Al Fayed but more generally a list of major defamation trials of the last 15 years.

One other tool is the Focus™ button, this is another way of refining a search and enables you to quickly search within a retrieved document.

Searching

Lexis has one basic search screen for all the databases. It is necessary to first choose the database you want to search, by using either the source directory or source shortcuts. It is possible to expand your search outside your original directory by choosing "explore" the source directory.

Searches in Lexis can be made by entering words in the search terms box, by using segment searches or both combined. Looking first at the search terms box searches, here Lexis relies heavily on Boolean operators like: "and", "or" and "not" as well as the truncator "!" and wildcards "*". Searches can also be narrowed down by using one of the "within" codes. For example, if you were looking for an article about the Internet and e-commerce, search for Internet w/10 e-commerce. Articles with those two words within 10 words of each other will be found, alternatively, you could look for words within the same sentence or paragraph. Another useful search tool is the ATLEAST or ATL search. This search enables you to specify how many times a word must appear.

I was trying to find the House of Lords transcript for the recent *Hamilton* v. *Al Fayed* libel trial. I searched: Hamilton w/5 Al Fayed. The first response was the transcript I was looking for reported in *The Times*, March 28. I followed this up with a search to look for all the cases Al Fayed had been involved in: ATL 5 (AL Fayed). This produced 21 cases starting with the Lonrho saga in the late 1980s. I tried several cases in the cases database and was very successful.

As stated above it is also possible to search by Segment, this is the same as a field search, *i.e.* you can specify what field you want to be searched, *i.e.* heading, catchwords, writtenby, etc. A segment search can also be combined with a search terms search.

The same principles apply to searches in the legislation and E.U. databases.

Subscription

Prices for access to U.K. Legal which gives unlimited access to all U.K. legal, U.K. news, commonwealth and E.U. Legal is approximately £595 per month for five users, with the price reducing per user the more there are.

It is also possible to subscribe on a pay as you go basis. This costs £50 per month plus a charge for each search, for instance to search the English cases database would cost £22.

Buy and use this service:

- For the really extensive database.
- For the accurate searching available.

Lawtel (http://www.interactive-lawyer.com)

Lawtel is part of the Centaur Group of companies and can be found at the Interactive Lawyer web site alongside The Lawyer and E.U. Interactive. The screens are simply laid out and there is a consistency of design across the databases. It is one of the simpler systems to get to grips with quickly.

Lawtel has more in common with Current Legal Information than with Lexis or Westlaw. Lawtel appears to be aimed more at keeping the busy practitioner on top of new developments in the law rather than facilitating in-depth research. Lawtel provides the lawyer with only as much information as they want and tries not to overload them with weighty judgments when a short synopsis will do. This principle is applied across the databases. Lawtel only covers U.K. law. A separate subscription to E.U. Interactive is needed to research E.U. law.

The simplicity and constancy of the screen on Lawtel make it very easy to locate the information you need, whether it is search tips or the coverage of the databases. On screen information is generally very concise and clear.

The use of hyperlinking in the case law and articles index is very good, this gives a more seamless product than some others.

One criticism would be that the quality and presentation of information provided for statute law is not as high as that for case law. Statute summaries are very brief and only give an indication of the contents of the statute. If the full text is available this is an unamended version. It is necessary to check the commencement and repeals section to see if a section is in force. There is also no hyperlinking to the amending provisions.

Content

Lawtel is made up of 10 basic databases, the daily update and the 24 specialist centres. Looking first at the daily update. This is a very simple to customise updating service. It provides on screen case summaries and references for cases, articles, statutory instruments and statutes in your chosen subject areas. It is updated every 24 hours.

The 10 databases are as follows: Case Law, P.I. Quantum Reports, Practice Directions, Articles Index, Research Bureau Answers, Statute Summaries, Statutory Instruments, Commencement and Repeals, Parliamentary Bills and Command Papers.

Looking in detail at the following:

Case Law

New case reports are added to the database often within hours of judgment from the House of Lords, Privy Council and Court of Appeal, Civil Division. There is also selected court coverage from the Court of Appeal, Criminal Division and the High Court and important judgments from some other courts and tribunals. The case law archive covers the same decisions as are reported in the All England Law Reports since 1980, the Independent Law Reports since 1986, the Times Law Reports since 1980 and the Weekly Law Reports since 1980. Lawtel also adds references from a number of specialist reports.

Articles Index

This is a searchable index with brief summaries of articles from approximately 50 legal publications. There are hypertext links to relevant cases and legislation.

Statutory Instruments

This searchable database includes all statutory instruments (and Northern Irish Statutory Rules) dating back to 1984. Details of every draft and official statutory instrument are provided within 24 hours of publication. For 1999 documents onwards it is also possible to see whether any Acts passed post-1999 have amended or revoked a particular statutory instrument together with hyperlinks to the relevant Acts.

Commencement and Repeals

Details of commencement dates and repeals are provided for all Acts on the database.

Statute Summaries

All Acts passed since 1984 are briefly summarised together with a list of the contents of the Act. From 1990 onwards it is possible to access the original text of the Act.

Specialist Centres

The specialist centres are all part of the package. They enable you to still have the broad Lawtel database but also to be able to focus your research on your practice area. Subjects covered include: personal injury, local government, intellectual property and civil procedure.

Tools Transcript Express

If the full text of a judgment or article is available you can order it on screen. There is an extra fee of approximately £8.50 per item. The document can be delivered by e-mail or fax in about 20 minutes.

Searching

I conducted the majority of my searches in the case law database though I did also search in the articles index and publications database both simply and successfully.

In the case law database I concentrated my searching on trying to find recent cases that had revisited the questions of foreseeability of damage raised in *Dorset Yacht* v. *Home Office* [1970] 1 A.C. 1004. I searched firstly for "Dorset Yacht" and found 11 hits where Dorset Yacht was mentioned including the Dorset Yacht case itself. In the case law database a search will initially give you a number of hits with a very brief description of the case. If you select one of the hits you will be given a longer case summary and for some cases the option of ordering the full judgment by Transcript Express. The hits are arranged in date order with the most recent first. The cases were all relevant and the search was effective in updating me on recent developments in this area. I did further searches to see if there were any other cases on foreseeablity. I searched for "negligen*" and "foreseeab* 2000". This gave me 22 hits of the most up to date case law on the subject.

One thing to be aware of when formulating a search is that the searching is against information contained in the databases, these contain summaries of the actual case, so your search will be limited to finding the words in the summaries and not the full text. If you bear this in mind when choosing your search words it should not be a problem.

Subscription

Subscription rates start at £600 to £700 per annum for a sole practitioner on a sliding scale upwards depending on the number of fee earners.

Buy and use this service:

- If you are a busy practitioner who needs to keep up to date but who doesn't have time for extensive research.
- For its simplicity of use.
- For the extensive hyperlinking between databases.
- For the excellent updating service.

EU Interactive (http://www.interactive-lawyer.com)

The E.U. law on Lawtel has been spun off into a separate product devoted to E.U. law. The service incorporates all the information from Spicers Centre for Europe. It includes an E.U. daily update, case law, legislation, articles index and background information on the E.U. as well as an E.U. Transcripts Express.

Buy and use this service:

- Because it has one of the best databases of E.U. law.
- To keep up to date with the E.U. daily update.

Justis Online (http://www.justis.com)

Justis Online offers a no frills service. Three searchable databases are provided: case law, European law and U.K. statutory instruments.

It is simple to log on and connection times were quite quick. I found the scrolling a bit unwieldy on my browser but otherwise no real complaints about the set up.

On the plus side the cases are presented on screen in a very easy to read format, exactly like a paper law report even with the original page numbering allowing for easier navigation. Also, the hyperlinking in the cases is very good, it is easy to flip backwards and forwards between your main case and those referred to in judgment.

A problem though for the novice user is the lack of information on screen. On the one hand this means that there is a clear uncluttered screen to work from but on the other hand it is not completely clear where to find essential information. For instance it states in the statutes database that statutory instruments can be searched but it is not clear from what date these S.I.s are available. It is in fact only from 1987 but this can only be found out by going to the "help" button, selecting Justis.com databases and then choosing S.I.s. The same problem arises with searching. There is no information on screen and no separate search button to give a brief overview of search techniques, again it is essential to press the "help" button and read the section on "search screen" before undertaking any searches. These are really only problems for the beginner as once you are familiar with the service, the actual content and the search engine become more important.

Content

Case Law

The Law Reports (1865–)

The Weekly Law Reports (1953–)

Industrial Cases (1972–)

Times Law Reports (1990–)

Lloyds Law Reports (1919–)

Law Reports Digest

The Law Reports Digests are really only applicable if you do not subscribe to the full package. If this is the case the Digests of The Law Reports and The Weeklies are available.

European Law

This consists of Celex and the Official Journal C Series. Celex is the computerised documentation system for the E.U. used by all the institutions that make up the Union. It includes European Legislation (1951–), Judgments and Orders (1951–) and Treaties (1953–). Celex with a basic searching service is available free at the Europa site (**http://europa.eu.int/celex**). If you take the Celex option from Justis you are paying for the better and quicker search facilities offered.

Statutes

This only contains statutory instruments from January 1987, at the moment.

Tools

A couple of useful features are provided. The document trail button provides a list of all the documents you have visited in your search session with direct links. The second is the J-Link service. If you download the software from on site and subscribe to Justis.com then the J-Link software enables hyperlinking from references in nearly all databases, word processing files, e-mails or web sites to the relevant document in the Justis Database. In essence you can attach all the original case reports and S.I.s to any report you write.

Searching

Searching can be by document reference, free text or fields.

When searching for Case Law Document Reference means Case Reference. For instance, 1978 Q.B. 490 will find *Jeffrey* v. *Black* very quickly. I found more problems using the free text search and the fields box's. I started off putting in as many keywords to the case as I could think of and got nowhere. I then checked the word indices to make sure the words I was using were in the database of searchable words. I still didn't get any hits. The trick I found was to use only one or two words in the free text section. "Less is more," definitely worked with this search engine. Searching for the words: police and search, Justis came up with two pages of cases including *Jeffrey* v. *Black*.

I had more immediate luck searching the European Law Database and was able to find numerous references to Factortame and European Court of Justice decisions that had considered this case in judgment.

Subscription

Subscriptions start at £250 per annum for an individual subscriber for The Times Law Reports up to £1750 per annum for The Law Reports including The Weekly law Reports and The Law Report Digest.

Buy and use this service:

- Because it is cheap.
- For the ease of reading material off the screen.
- For the good hyperlnking between cases.

Current Legal Information (http://www.smlawpub.co.uk)

Current Legal Information is to be found hidden away on the main Sweet and Maxwell site under online services. It contains some very valuable material for the legal practitioner and law student. In its paper form, once you have got used to its format, it is the quickest and easiest way to update any legal research. It would seem to be the type of information that could easily be transferred to an online format by using hyperlinks between the Citators and Current Law. Unfortunately, this opportunity has not been taken yet and it is at the time of writing slow and unwieldy to use. The information on screen for the Case and Legislation Citators could easily be improved. At the moment, on entering these databases you are presented with search boxes with no explanation of the function or workings of the Citators. This information can be found, but only by accessing "help". Even given these criticisms it is still the source of some information that just cannot be found elsewhere and so lets hope that the "enhancements" in the pipeline sort out the problems.

Content

Current Legal Information is made up of the following eight databases:

Current Law Cases

Current Law Cases is an index of cases and case summaries. It is very comprehensive including all cases reported in over 70 reports, the electronic database going back to 1986. It also has selected cases from High Court transcripts and for personal injury specialists, the Measure of Damages Cases sent in from the lower courts.

Badger Grey Paper Index

This index contains short summaries of public information of relevance to the legal profession. This includes statutory instruments, Bills, guidance notes, press releases, White Papers, Green Papers and European Commission COMdocs. There are links in the summaries to external websites where the full text of listed documents can be found.

Legal Journals Index

This is an index to every significant legal journal article published since 1986. It includes very brief details of the content of the article and information on where the full text of the article can be found.

Financial Journals Index

The Financial Journals Index is an index to articles appearing in U.K. and European Financial Journals back to 1992. Again it includes brief information on the content and where the full text can be found.

Case Citator

The Case Citator is a guide to developments in case law since 1989. The Citator details the citations of published cases and gives information on where cases have been judicially considered. The year and paragraph number of the abstract in Current Law is also stated but given that there is no hyperlinking between the two databases and that the Current Law database cannot be accessed by paragraph number then this information is not much use.

Legislation Citator

The Legislation Citator provides a guide to changes in statutes and details instances where statutes have been judicially considered from 1989 as well as giving details of any statutory instruments made

131

under the Acts provisions. Unfortunately, when an Act has been referred to or amended by another Act only the year and chapter number of the Act is given, as there is no index of Acts by year and chapter number on site, this information is not particularly useful. There is also no hyperlinking to Current Law or the Case Citator.

Inns of Court Catalogues

These are indices of contents of the libraries of the Inns of Court.

Casecheck

Subscribers to Current Legal Information have now been given access to the Casecheck facility. This is a weekly index of all judgements of the House of Lords, Privy Council, Court of Appeal, High Court and Crown Office. This includes a summary of the findings in the case.

Searching

All the databases are separate with their own search facilities but the same system is employed by each. Searching can be by natural language with Boolean operators like "and" and "not" or by using fields to narrow down your search to particular courts, years, etc. There are short but clear instructions on site to help with searching techniques. I conducted several searches across the databases. I found the searches in Current Law to be very slow.

In the Case Citator I was trying to get full references for the Jonathan Aitken saga and in particular references for the original case against Granada Television. I tried searching against the case name and came up blank. Far more effective is to search for the names in the case name joined with "and". This method came up trumps with; *Aitken* v. *Preston* (joined with *Aitken* v. *Granada Television Limited*) [1997] E.M.L.R. 415, digested at 97/2030 of Current Law.

Subscription

Prices start for the full service at £635 per annum for a sole practitioner rising upwards with the number of partners.

Buy and use this service:

- For the reports on quantum if you are a P.I. specialist.
- For the citators if you do not have an alternative electronic updating facility.

Are You Ready for the Web?

Having read the whole section on Finding Law Online and Legal Research Online check out the following points to see if you are truly ready:

- Have you checked out some new sites in your practice area since reading this book?
- Have you bookmarked at least your top five legal research sites?
- Do you do all your legal research online?
- Do you know where to find the best sites to research your legal speciality?

Part C: The Best of the Rest: Other Legal Sites

Part C is focused on all the legal sites that are not primarily concerned with black letter law. The sites that provide gateways to other legal sites, that give up to date legal news or point the way to a new job. There are hundreds and lots more coming. I have covered the ones I think are the best or the most prominent, but you will find others.

CHAPTER ONE

LEGAL PORTALS

Portals are web sites offering a gateway to information on the Internet. A major legal portal should offer links to all major areas of law, to firms, chambers, universities, journals, legislation and cases on the Internet and most importantly be easy to use. In this section I have divided the legal portals into two types. The first type I have looked at is the true legal portal and the second is the online legal community: part portal but usually offering more than just links to legal pages. In this section I use the words legal portal to include both types.

For lawyers the usefulness of a legal portal is in having a whole collection of legal links on the one page. It saves time and hassle. The legal news, links to sources of case law and legislation and articles and comment on the law can all be found in one place.

The whole point of a portal is to make dealing with the huge amount of information on the Internet manageable. It should be possible to open the portal as your homepage and use it as your base for researching law on the web.

Legal portals didn't exist at all a couple of years ago but new ones are appearing all the time. I have looked at the ones that I think are the best. After reading this section I would suggest that half an hour could be valuably spent browsing through the different portals in order to decide which one most fits your needs for content and ease of use. I would recommend Delia Venables site for the sheer quantity of information. I have also found the Lawlinks site compiled by Sarah Carter at Kent University to be very useful. Of the online legal communities I find LawZone very consumer friendly and The Jurist site is excellent for news.

Legal Portals

The Bailii Project (http://www.bailii.org)

The Bailii project is not setting itself up as a legal portal but that is essentially how it operates. In time when new law is added there will be links to all the case law and statute law on the Internet from the five jurisdictions. All of this being searchable and hyperlinked. If this was all that was on site it probably would not make it as a portal but there is also content from the AustIII site (**http://www.austlii.edu.au**). This can be accessed through the world law button. This takes us to links to e-journals, law libraries, international law and international institutions. Entries tend to have a slight Aussie emphasis. The material available also includes Internet law sites from countries all over the world from Project Dial (**http://www.austlii.edu.au/dial/**). Project Dial is a project funded by the Asian Development Bank aimed at making it easier to find legislation related materials on the Internet with the particular aim of helping lawyers and legal drafting personnel in developing Asian and Pacific countries access comparative law.

Infolaw (http://www.infolaw.co.uk)

The Infolaw portal is billed as the "Information for Lawyers Limited's Gateway to the U.K. Legal Internet". The site is simply set out and is very easy to use, the visitor is not bombarded by graphics or twirling words as at some other sites. The list of available information starts off with Nick's page—highlighting the fact that the page is maintained by Nick Holmes, the man behind Information for Lawyers Limited. This also points out another fact about U.K. portals, the fact that they often stem from the interest of an individual that has grown and grown. See Delia Venables site below or Laurie West-Knights' (**http://www.lawonline.cc**).

Nick's page is essentially a list of legal topics with links to articles written by Nick Holmes and previously published elsewhere. If you are interested in the Internet there are some interesting articles to read. If not skip this and move on to another category in the list that interests you. The other categories include law firms, chambers, barristers, government, parliament and the courts, legal resources and goods and services. Some categories have more links than others. The list of law firms is good, rather startlingly highlighting those firms among the top 500 that don't yet have a web site. Otherwise I found the list of legal resources by topic helpful.

Delia Venables (http://www.venables.co.uk)

Delia Venables is a computer consultant who advises law firms on information technology and also runs this well known web site. It is the most comprehensive collection of links currently available for U.K. and Irish law. The site includes listings for the following:

- Legal sites and resources in the U.K.
- Irish legal sites.
- Most significant new sites.
- Online services from legal publishers.
- Solicitors in England.
- Barristers in England.
- Selling legal services online.
- Legal newspapers and journals.

Delia Venables also offers Internet Studies for Lawyers and an Internet Newsletter for Lawyers (both by subscription). Also, if you think your firm's web site needs a workout Delia offers a service where your web site is put through its paces on different browsers and generally assessed.

Lawlinks (http://www.library.ac.uk/library/netinfo/intnsubg/lawlinks.htm)

More commonly known as Lawlinks. This portal or annotated list of web sites as it sells itself is the work of Sarah Carter of the University of Kent Law library. It is a straightforward list of different categories like gateways to legal information, subscription services, electronic legal journals and U.K. legal resources. Under each category you will find an extensive list of annotated links. A site that needs bookmarking as it would be impossible to remember the URL.

Connecting Legal (http://www.connectinglegal.com)

Connecting Legal comes from Waterlow's the legal services company. This is a simple, straightforward one page portal with lots of information on legal services, law courses, domain names, legal news, etc. It was the only place where I could easily find listings for law costs draftsmen, a legal service that seems to have slipped through a lot of other nets.

Access to Law (http://www.accesstolaw.org)

Access to Law is one of the most accessible portals. It is set out in a very simple to use format, is easy to read and fast to use. The information on site is split up into U.K., European, USA and Canadian or Australian and New Zealand legal materials. Sticking to the U.K. page categories you can search from among others: legislation, secondary legislation, cases and e-journals. One helpful feature of the site is that each link is annotated. This makes it easier to choose links that are going to be really helpful rather than going off on a wild goose chase. There is only one problem with the Access to Law site and that is the quantity of information available. Again this is quite a new site so matters may improve as more links are added but, unfortunately, when I checked the new sites added button I was informed that no new sites had been added in the last 30 days. This did not exactly inspire confidence that people were beavering away to bring the quantity of information accessible on the site up to scratch with the quality of the rest of the features.

Access to Law is a product of Go Interactive a well known Internet company and web designer and as such the site also offers other Internet services. One service offered is that of Internet Service Provider (ISP) just download the software from the site to use them as your free ISP. Another Internet service on site is the possibility to search the registers of domain names to see if your name of choice is available. If it is you can begin the process of registering your domain name on site.

Findlaw (http://findlaw.com) and Hieros Gamos (http://www.hg.org)

The Findlaw and Hieros Gamos sites are both massive and very comprehensive. They are American sites with some U.K. links but essentially for U.S. lawyers or for U.K. lawyers trying to research U.S. law. There is more information about them on p. 89 in the International Law section.

Online Legal Communities

The distinction between a legal portal and an online legal community is a matter of emphasis. A portal is aiming to provide access to information while often offering other services as well. An online legal community offers something more intangible: membership of a group, whilst also offering links to legal sites and providing and selling services. An online legal communities use to any individual lawyer is the same as for any other portal. Do you need the services offered? Have a look at some of the sites and see.

LawZone (http://www.lawzone.co.uk)

LawZone, unlike a lot of other sites, feels as if it was designed for the Internet. It is quick and couldn't be simpler to navigate. It bills itself as an "online legal community providing daily news, information, resources and practice management tips." LawZone as a concept could not have existed even two years ago, there were simply not enough lawyers online, but now it is growing (like a lot of other legal sites) at a phenomenal rate as lawyers catch on to the virtual world. LawZone is an interactive site, input is welcome whether it is voting in a poll, hosting or attending an online workshop or adding new links.

At the time of writing, LawZone provided a range of general news, legal news and services. The legal news is presented as a series of

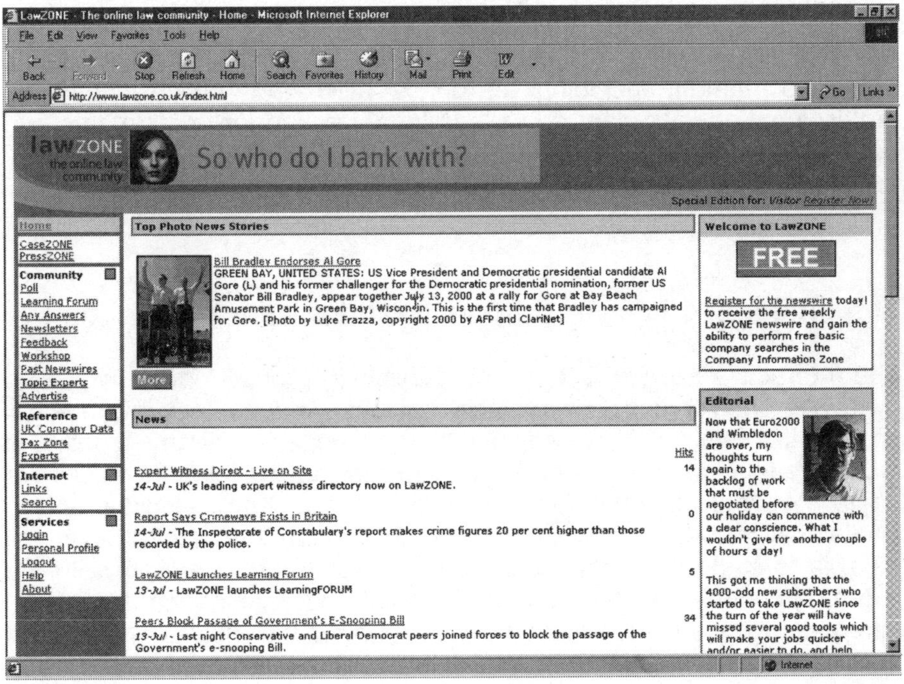

short summaries, if you are tempted to know more, link to the full story. If you do follow up and read the whole story, relevant related stories are there at the click of a mouse.

The CaseZone gives brief case summaries and court news and the TaxZone news, law and updates on tax matters. The PressZone allows companies and firms to post their press releases.

Other services on offer include:

- Weekly online workshops with topic specialists.
- A question and answer area where lawyers, students and any other interested parties can post questions that need answering. A brief perusal found a few students wanting some help with their homework as well as lawyers with interesting problems hoping for some input.
- Company and director searches through a link on site, payment is on an "as you go" basis.
- A local area search engine. This search engine can be used to search relevant legal sites.
- A shopping mall: to buy your legal books and sundries.

Plans in the pipeline include a StudentZone for all things studenty, online recruitment including an online milkround, online continuing professional development as well as legal training for accountants and accountancy training for lawyers. From the feel of it that is probably just the start of it, there will undoubtedly be more to come.

The Interactive Lawyer (http://www.interactivelawyer.com)

The Interactive Lawyer is from the publishing group Centaur who also own The Lawyer and Lawtel. It is obviously hoped that lawyers will choose the Interactive Lawyer as their homepage thereby creating a captive audience of lawyers for all their products. Interactive Lawyer offers 24 specialist centres on areas of law from employment to intellectual property. The intention being that an individual lawyer will be able to customise their Interactive Lawyer to provide them with the information they need and not be distracted by unnecessary legal information. This customisation of services for the individual lawyer is part of a growing trend within the Internet as a whole is only just starting to make a mark in the world of legal web sites.

Access to the Interactive Lawyer site will be free as will continued access to The Lawyer. Lawtel and EU Interactive will continue to be subscription sites linked through the Interactive Lawyer homepage.

Other content includes:

- An online legal bookshop.
- A diary of legal events.
- Online debates.
- Specialist legal centres.

The Jurist (http://www.law.cam.ac.uk/jurist/index.htm)

The Jurist is an online legal community aimed at law lecturers and students. It is part of a network of Jurist sites in the USA, Canada and Australia. The Jurist site has one of the best news sections I have seen anywhere on the Web. The latest legal news is there, but so is Breaking News, updated every five minutes and audio or video newscasts from the BBC and IRN: a really good resource. The Jurist also has content that is purely legal. There are links to all the law schools in the U.K. and articles by U.K. law teachers and web pages by law teachers on course related topics. As well as a bulletin board site for faculty and students. The reference desk button takes you to links to the courts, government, legal research sites and links to academic job sites.

Elexica (http://www.elexica.com)

Elexica could not be called a portal because there are just not enough links to other sites. Elexica is an off shoot of Simmons and Simmons. It states that it is an "online legal resource by lawyers for lawyers with content from Simmons and Simmons". The site looks very expensive with lots of graphics. It is quite hard to navigate. When I visited there was a problem with scrolling down lists which hopefully has been sorted by now. The content provided by Simmons and Simmons was not very extensive at the time, though it has to be said this was shortly after its launch and the site has probably expanded by now. The content included contract checklists for different areas and the Communications Regulations Monitoring Service, a publication highlighting legal, regulatory and policy developments in the communications industry. There is also an E.U. diary giving weekly notice of proceedings in the E.U. and a virtual library that can be searched by topic. The resources of the library when I visited were pretty limited, three links under Internet!

Like Access to Law, Elexica is also aiming to be an Internet Service Provider with the ability to download on site and thereby build up a customer base made up entirely of lawyers!

Lawyers On Line (http://lawyersonline.co.uk)

Lawyers On Line appears to sell itself primarily as a dedicated Internet Service Provider for lawyers. They want you to choose lawyers online to provide your access to the Internet. The site itself is quite complex with lots of twirling words. This said it is relatively easy to navigate around and I found it to be quite fast. Other services offered include Continuing Professional Development by subscription, a web site design service and a secure e-mail service. There are also a limited number of links to government sites, libraries, experts, recruitment sites and some specialist areas. One service that is offered, and I am surprised is not offered more widely elsewhere, is the barrister referral system. A solicitor simply fills in a form online giving details of their case and the type of barrister they require. This information is then sent to 200 barristers clerks around the country who are expected to tender for the business.

CHAPTER TWO

LEGAL FORMS AND SERVICES

The majority of this section covers the provision of services to lawyers by the government and private companies including the provision of legal forms online.

I have also included at the end of this section a very small selection of legal service providers on the web. These are the competition for the high street firm of the future, conveyancing, wills, divorces, etc., the web can often provide a cheaper alternative than the high street solicitor. The Internet understands that information is power. Once consumers are given easy access to free legal information they are in the position to choose what type of legal service they want or need. A lot of people appreciate the fact that they don't need a custom built will or employment contract and that the standard one will do just fine. This doesn't necessarily mean that there will be fewer lawyers in the future but maybe it does mean that a few thousand of them might find themselves in call centres answering telephones and online enquiries as employees of the large online law providers.

It is obviously a good idea for lawyers to read this section but it should be essential reading for practice managers and legal secretaries.

Forms

There are a lot of forms available on the Internet and they are often free. It is one of those areas where the Internet comes into its own. Already the stationery cupboard is becoming redundant.

As mentioned before, the majority of forms are published on the Internet in pdf or Portable Document Format. In order for your computer to be able to read these forms you will need to download the Adobe Acrobat Reader Software. This is available free at the

Adobe Corporation web site (**http://www.adobe.com**). If you go to the Adobe site it is simply a matter of clicking on a couple of links to specify the type of computer and program you have and then waiting for the software to download. Once it has been downloaded and stored on your computer you will be able to read all documents stored in pdf.

The other format you are likely to come across is Capsoft U.K.'s Hotdocs. In particular this is used for the Legal Aid Board Forms. Again, you will need to download software to be able to read these forms. This time you will need to download the Hotdoc's Player (**http://www.hotdocs.co.uk**) again available free.

Government Forms

The Court Service (**http://www.courtservice.gov.uk**)

The plan for the court service is to get "all possible" forms online, that is approximately 233. Those that have to be generated by the court obviously can't be put online. The forms are in pdf and are interactive, *i.e.* you can complete them on screen, print them off and send to the relevant court. It is not possible yet to file forms online, but it is only a matter of time. The court service told me that they hoped this would be in place by, at the latest, 2008.

The Land Registry (**http://www.landreg.gov.uk**)

Land registry forms are in pdf (see above) and are available for downloading.

Insolvency Service (**http://www.insolvency.gov.uk**)

The insolvency service provides the statutory insolvency forms for downloading and printing off.

Patent Office **(http://www.patent.gov.uk)**

The Patent Office site forms are all in pdf, see above. The forms available include patent, trade-mark, design and design rights and supplementary protection. Explanatory notes can also be downloaded with each form.

Legal Aid Forms **(http://www.lawsociety.hotdocs.co.uk)**

The legal services commission forms provided by the Law Society are in the HotDocs format. They are interactive and are programmed to remember information so it doesn't have to be typed in twice.

Inland Revenue **(http://www.inlandrevenue.gov.uk)**

A selection of the most commonly required Inland Revenue tax forms for 1999/2000 are available for downloading. These include self assessment tax returns, corporation tax self assessment, PAYE and NIC employers annual pack and inheritance tax 200 and notes. Other forms need to be requested from a tax office. The forms are in pdf (see above) but they cannot be filled in online.

Companies House **(http://www.companies-house.gov.uk)**

A limited number of Companies House forms are available in pdf (see above). They are interactive and can therefore be completed simply online and printed off.

Home Office **(http://www.homeoffice.gov.uk)**

The Home Office web site collects together all the forms from different parts of the site. This makes them very easy to find. The forms are in pdf and include immigration forms, animal scientific procedure forms and drugs forms.

147

Department of Education and Employment (http://www.dfee.gov.uk)

The Dfee site has forms necessary to apply for work permits. These are held in Word 7 format. If your browser does not support this, software is available on site for downloading.

Her Majesty's Custom and Excise (http://www.hmce.gov.uk)

The Custom and Excise site has an extensive selection of forms available in pdf (see above).

Publishers Forms

The majority of legal form publishers have some presence on the Internet as well as some new entrants who spotted a gap in the market. But with the growth of government forms readily and freely available on the Internet a little bit more needs to be provided.

Everyform (http://www.everyform.net)

Everyform provides all the forms from the government sites in one place and all in the same Hotdocs format. The forms are free, though there is a deluxe service with e-mail notification of new developments for £100 per annum. If you used forms regularly from different government departments Everyform would save the hassle of flipping between sites.

Oyez Straker (http://www.oyeznet.co.uk)

At the time of writing, Oyez were slightly behind the pack in not yet having an online capability. But Oyez are just about to go live with their online forms service; formslink. This promises to be a full forms service available from their web site. The service will be subscription based.

Statplus (http://www.statplus.co.uk)

Statplus offers laserform electronic law forms. These online forms can be purchased or rented in packs to reflect key subject areas of legal practice. The range available is limited compared to those that can be ordered online and sent by post.

Proforma Forms (http://www.proformaforms.co.uk)

Proforma forms appear to be an offshoot of Nick Holmes's Infolaw legal portal. It is not completely clear from the web site what forms are available online at this time.

Legal Services on the Internet

There are numerous providers of legal services on the Web helping lawyers in their daily work. The biggest by far is the Government. The Government provides a lot of the old services but by using the technology of the Internet they are able to deliver them, hopefully, in a new and better way. The non-government sites I have listed essentially use the Internet as a glorified yellow pages. This is perfect when that is what you need to find an expert or a costs draftsmen.

Government Services

- HM Customs and Excise (**http://www.hmce.gov.uk**) propose to offer a discount to all businesses that file their quarterly VAT returns electronically.

- Inland revenue (**http://www.inlandrevenue.gov.uk**) now allows the filing of self-assessment tax returns online and if you pay any tax due on time you will get a discount.

- Insolvency service (**http://www.insolvency.gov.uk**). The disqualified directors hotline has been extended to the Internet, fill a form in online to report a disqualified director caught trading. Searchable databases of official receivers and insolvency practitioners are also available.

- HM land registry (**http://www.landreg.gov.uk**) provides the direct access service for land registry credit account holders. This provides instant access to the computerised land register enabling you to view titles on screen, order office copies, lodge official searches and print hard copies from your screen. It is also proposed that a land charges search facility will be offered online to direct access users.

The land registry has also been involved in a pilot project with the Swindon and Stroud Building Society and the Nationwide Building Society to develop the Electronic Notification of Discharge (ENDs) facility. Since the introduction of ENDs participating building societies have been able to electronically notify the land registry that a charge or mortgage has been discharged. More lenders are coming online and, in the not too distant future, form DS1 will be no more!

- Companies House (**http://www.companies-house.gov.uk**) offers three different services over the Internet. First, Companies House permits electronic filing of documents over the Companies House extranet. The documents are automatically validated for compliance before a notice of acceptance is issued. Secondly, Companies House Direct provides a subscription search service. There is an intitial registration fee of £50 and a small charge per document. It is necessary to obtain free image viewing software from Companies House to use the system. Thirdly, Companies House Monitor is a service that enables you, for a fee, to register your interest in a named company. As soon as any documents are filed for this company a copy will be e-mailed to you.

- Patent Office (**http://www.patent.gov.uk**). The Patent Office offers a selection of search services for anyone interested. The Designs Register can be searched to establish whether a design registration is in force and the Designs Image Search Service allows you to search through on screen images of registered designs together with bibliographic information on the designer. For patents **esp@cenet** provides an interface to the U.K. Patent Office, European Patent Office and other European National Patent Offices. The Patent Status Information service allows online checking of a patent's priority, filing dates and owner. Lastly, facilities are available to search the Trade Marks register and to find the correct class of goods or services you need to specify when applying to register a trademark.

Non-Government Services

Expert witnesses

There are numerous registers of expert witnesses online. One of the longest established and most comprehensive is JS Publishing's Register of expert witnesses (**http://www.jspubs.com**). Details of over 3000 experienced expert witnesses are held online in a fully searchable database. It is necessary to register on site to make full use of the directory.

The Academy of Experts (**http://www.academey-experts.org**) is an organisation for the education and promotion of expert witnesses. To become a member an expert witness must be accepted by the Academy as suitably qualified in their profession. The Academy maintains a searchable register of their experts.

Private Investigators

Lawyers sometimes need the assistance of a professional private investigator and like everything else they can find them and instruct them easily on the Internet. Safeguard Investigations Limited (**http://www.safeguard-investigations.ltd.uk**) specialises in covert surveillance work for lawyers and others, while Global Investigation Services (**http://www.ukprivateinvestigators.com**) will undertake people searches and a broad range of other investigative services.

Costs Draftsmen

A lot of firms of costs draftsmen have sites, for instance, Wigg and Co. (**http://wigg.co.uk**) and Rigby and Co. (**http://www.rigby.co.uk**) both have simple web sites. Taking the use of the Internet a little further Legalex Cost Drafting Service of Colchester (**http://www.legalex.co.uk**) offers clients access to data and progress reports on their files over the Internet through a system of password protected web pages.

Online Law Providers

Every lawyer, but particularly those in private practice, should visit these sites to see what the competition is doing and maybe to borrow some ideas.

Desktop Lawyer **(http://www.desktoplawyer.net)**

Desktop Lawyer is an impressive online legal services site. Using Rapidocs software, Desktop Lawyer is able to create, from questions asked and answers given, an individually tailored legal document. Telephone legal support at £1.50 per minute is available to help with the assembly of the legal document and to check that the document is accurate and appropriate. Documents available range from commercial contracts and partnership agreements to undefended divorces and powers of attorney. Prices per document start as low as £2.99 for a letter to request medical records to £59.99 for the undefended Divorce pack. Desktop Lawyer also provides an online conveyancing service. With the further distribution of the Rapidocs software to firms in the Direct Law Network (**http:c//www. directlaw.co.uk**) and to other providers like Freeserve (**http:// www.freeserve.com**) and Virgin (**http://www.virginbiz.net**) it seems that a lot of us are going to be dealing with Desktop Lawyer products in one way or another.

It has to be remembered that for every will, power of attorney, letter or contract drafted one less client is using a traditional high street practice. These lost clients are obtaining simple legal services quicker and cheaper than they previously thought possible and are no doubt telling all their friends.

Lawrights **(http://www.lawrights.co.uk)**

Lawrights aims to provide concise and independent legal information for consumers and businesses and to sell some of their legal services along the way. Advice is provided on a lot of topics from employment to personal injury by way of a series of questions and answers and factsheets. Services provided include Conveyancing Direct offered in association with the National Solicitors Network. Conveyancing Direct offers an e-mail based service or a personal referral service. Lawrights sells a limited range of legal documents online, prices are reasonable at £30 for an employment contract or only £4 for a lottery syndicate agreement. Aspiring e-entrepreneurs can also buy on site a pack of documents to get them up and running. Free online assistance is offered for completing any documents and a telephone legal advice line at £1.50 per minute is also available, this seems to be very much the going rate.

(c) Epoch Software Holdings Plc 1999-2000

Wills Wizard (http://www.willswizard.com)

The Wills Wizard is solicitor Phillip Gegan, his site offers advice, information and an Easyform questionnaire to assist in will preparation, wills costing £30 each. The Wills Wizard also offers free telephone back up when there is a problem.

Divorce Online (http://www.divorce-online.co.uk)

Another specialist service is Divorce Online this provides divorce packages from £60. This service is not as yet a truly online service as the documents are merely e-mailed or sent to the recipient for completion.

CHAPTER THREE

LEGAL NEWS AND VIEWS

Lawyers need legal news. It might be the announcement of a new government initiative, the details of the budget or just who has moved to what firm from where. Luckily it is easy to keep up to date with news on the Internet. The major legal news magazines have online editions as do some newcomers. It is interesting to watch the slow move away from publishing paper versions on the Internet towards a type of publishing that takes advantage of the new technology. The new publications are just beginning to use the interactive features of the Internet. In some cases enabling the reader to customize their e-zine in others to follow up news stories with links to related stories. My favourites are the new look Law Society Gazette and for a quick read LawZone.

The Internet, because of the very low costs of distribution, is also a good medium for distributing titles with small specialist readerships. I have included a few of these in this section, however, there are a lot more. They can usually be found at the sites of the major legal publishers, law firms or linked from specialist sites.

In the last part I examine general news resources on the Internet. These are excellent and I have bookmarked The BBC, The Financial Times and The Jurist.

Legal News

The Law Society Gazette (http://www.lawgazette.co.uk)

The Gazette online is an attractive easy to use and interactive legal news magazine. One interactive element is the bespoke content editor enabling you to specify your areas of interest. The site will store this information for when future visits. Your homepage at the online

Gazette will then be adapted to reflect these interests, helping you get straight to the legal areas or stories that interest you most. The rest of the magazine is still there just buried a little deeper.

Another interactive element is the job tracker, just enter your criteria for a job, the Gazette will search its databanks for a suitable position. When a vacancy matching your criteria is found this will be posted on your homepage saving you the trawl through the jobs pages.

General content is similar to the paper version and of a consistent quality. It includes extensive legal news, editorial, features and practice as well as the situations vacant site. This new site also promises better search facilities for searching the archives. The archives go back as far as 1997 and can be a very useful research tool.

The Lawyer (http://www.interactive-lawyer.com)

The Lawyer can now be found on the homepage of the Interactive Lawyer, no doubt hoping to entice the regular online readership of The Lawyer to use the other services available through the Interactive Lawyer online community.

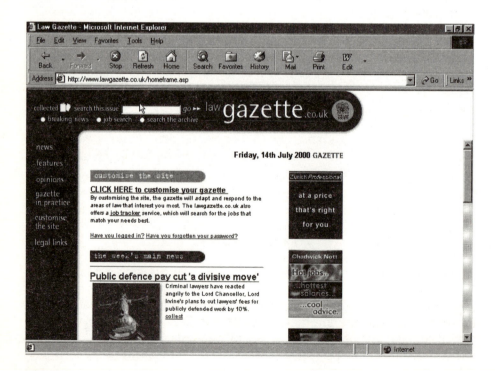

The Lawyer is to be found under a number of different buttons, such as news, deals, opinion and profiles. It is all there just not all under one heading. Given that, it is surprising that The Lawyer Online manages to maintain the look and feel of the paper version. Maybe by sticking to the original format some opportunities offered by interactive Internet publishing have been lost. But that said it is clearly set out and easy to use and given its position on the Interactive Lawyer site maybe soon The Lawyer will be a bit more interactive too

Other content:

- Company searches: links to Equifax and Perfect Information.
- Directories: Legal Technology Directory, Waterlow Solicitors Directory, Legal Recruitment Consultancies.
- Jobs Online: A comprehensive legal recruitment site, searchable by sector, practice, area, PQE or region.

LawZone (http://www.lawzone.co.uk)

As well as offering the facilities of an Online Legal Community (see p. 141) LawZone has a good news section offering general news stories and legal news easily accessed with links to related stories covered by LawZone. If you register at the LawZone site you will receive by e-mail the weekly LawZone newswire.

InBrief (http://www.inbrief.co.uk)

InBrief is a monthly guide to law and lawyers. The online version contains a selection of InBriefs lead stories from current issue. The stories are more views than news with not much of the "this partner moved here and that partner moved there" stories, common in The Lawyer. Other information on site includes a Bluffer's Guide to London Firms. This gives a brief run down of the major firms, who is doing what and who to watch, etc. It is interesting but some of the copy seemed a bit dated. There is a jobs site but it is not nearly as extensive as The Lawyer's online recruitment site.

InBrief does have a sister site, The World Legal forum with a link from InBrief. The World Legal Forum Site (**http://www.world legalforum.co.uk**) aims to provide information on law and law firms in a variety of countries. Information given includes an introduction explaining the structure of the law profession plus articles with the latest legal news, articles by top firms, a guide to recommended firms, surveys of major firms and travel advice. For some countries this is a really useful resource but the information given was often incomplete, it was very much a case of potluck depending on the country. The site as a whole seemed to be a work in progress so maybe in a few months time it will be more comprehensive and up to date.

LegalWeek.Net (http://www.lwk.co.uk)

Legal Week is another general legal news magazine. It contains some general news stories but at this stage it has to be said that there does not appear to be a lot of news going on to this site. There is another section called notices dealing with who is moving where. An area of the site due to be launched soon is the Newsletters area where it will be possible to search different solicitors firms' online publications. There is also a job site.

News Direct (http://www.butterworths.co.uk/newsdirect)

Butterworths online legal newspaper is to be found in an offshoot of their main site. News Direct does not appear to aim to compete with the major legal news providers. It provides some legal news and some comment on areas of interest to lawyers but is not nearly as comprehensive as others, but it is easy to read and a quick way to get the main stories.

Specialist News

PLC and European Counsel (htp://www.plcinfo.com)

PLC Publications provides a subscription based information service based on the European Counsel and PLC magazines. The publication is aimed at corporate and commercial lawyers. The archive has more than 11,000 searchable legal articles, precedents and checklists. The cost starts at £120 for one user.

Monitor Press (http://www.monitorpress.co.uk)

Monitor Press produce a large range of legal newsletters and reports including corporate briefing, litigation letter, conditional, contingency and other alternative fee arrangements and medical negligence and clinical risk. A sample is usually available to view online with facilities for ordering the hard copy.

Electronic Newsletters

Sweet and Maxwell (**http://www.sweetandmaxwell.co.uk**) produce a lot of online newsletters, some like European Union News are only available to subscribers while others like In Competition Online are free. Otherwise the majority of newsletters are produced by firms as a service to clients or potential clients, for instance, Bird and Bird (**http://twobirds.com**) produce several regular newsletters including the IT Law Bulletin, Property Update, European Update and Biosciences Update. Blake Lapthorn (**http://www.blakelapthorn. co.uk**) publish newsletters on, among other issues, leisure and child law. If you chose to do minimal research among solicitors that specialise in your area of practice you could very simply register and receive regular e-mail updates on the area of your choice.

General News

General news sites can be as useful to the lawyer as the specialist sites and are in any event essential reading. If you want to watch the news on your screen or listen to the radio you will usually need to download software. There are lots of different types. One of the best known is the Real Player software, found at **http://www.real.com**. Once you have downloaded the software on to your computer you can watch the BBC or listen to the world service or a myriad of other stations. Watch out though, your picture quality might not be brilliant, it will depend largely upon the speed of your connection and how up to date your computer is. If you are going to be watching a lot of videos you might need to upgrade your computer or install a video card into your machine.

Law on the Internet

Here are some of the essential news sites:

- The BBC (**http://www.bbc.co.uk/news**) web sites are the most visited in the U.K. It is easy to understand why. The news section is packed with information with the ability to plug into audio or watch the news on a video link.

- *The Times* (**http://www.the-times.co.uk**) has all the features of its paper cousin as well as some extras. In particular it has NewsFirst which is its breaking news service. This is in fact the easiest way to get straight to all the main daily news stories. There is also a new section called Inter//face 2000 for all those interested in the new economy. There are search facilities on site.

- *The Financial Times* (**http://www.ft.com**) has a clear attractive look. It is one of the only heavily branded online newspapers and I would have thought it would be an essential bookmark for anyone in the City or doing City business. It is also very easy to read and to search. Searches can include not only ft.com but also the web and ft.com's global archive of over 3000 business sources.

- *The Guardian* (**http://www.guardianunlimited.co.uk**) is very readable, clearly presented with good use of colour. It is noticeably different to the newspaper. If you don't get the chance to read the paper in the morning you can have a quick guide to today's news e-mailed to you daily by filling in your e-mail address. *The Observer* is thrown in as well for good measure.

- *The Daily Telegraph* (**http://www.telegraph.co.uk**) is very colourful with adverts and lots of gizmos on screen. A useful technique used is to include relevant external links alongside news stories.

- *The Jurist* (**http://www.law.cam.ac.uk/jurist/index.htm**) has a good news site including legal news and general news. The general news includes breaking news updated every five minutes as well as audio and video links to BBC and IRN news broadcasts.

- *The Paperboy* (**http://www.thepaperboy.com**) is a useful bookmark to have. The site is essentially a smart well managed set of links to over 3821 newspapers in 133 countries. If you want to read the *Jakarta Post, Irish Times* or *Herts Advertiser* they are all there. All local U.K. newspapers that are online are listed, U.K. national papers can be found by name and are listed under London.

CHAPTER FOUR

LAW FIRMS

This section is going to look at two quite separate issues. First, it is going to look briefly at how to get a firm set up on the web. In doing this it is going to look at why a firm needs a web site and how to go about getting one. I have also included some examples of good sites and ideas on content. There is also a short section on marketing and information on where to list the site.

The second issue is going to look at firms that are already providing legal services on the web, what services they are providing and, where possible, what developments are in the pipeline.

How to Set Your Firm up on the Internet

Why Do You Need a Web Site?

The cry I often hear from the unreformed lawyer is that they don't have the time and, anyway, even if they did a good lawyer is a good lawyer irrespective of the Internet, Intranets, Extranets or web sites. This may well be true but no one is going to want to use this good lawyer unless they can provide these good lawyering skills together with the best technology because a lot of the other good lawyers will be offering both.

Another reason why a law firm's web site and Internet strategy is of crucial importance is the ability of a firm to attract potential employees. These employees are going to look at the web site and ask about the firm's Internet strategy. If they are not doing this now they will be very soon. An employee wants to have confidence in the future of the business that they are entrusting their career with. If a firm is getting left behind in their use of new technology what does this say about the attitudes of the firm towards the future? On the other hand it is also important that potential employees are familiar with the issues themselves. It is not enough to just have the legal skills. In the future it is also going to be necessary to think about how technology is going to assist you as a lawyer in delivering those skills to your clients.

How Do You Set Up a Web Site?

This is a job for the professionals. You will need to find and instruct a web designer to design your web site. One of the best ways to do this is by finding sites you like the look of (see below for some examples) and find out who designed them or, alternatively, from recommendations from other firms. If none of these routes prove successful, look for web designers in the directories section at The Interactive Lawyer (**http://www.interactive-lawyer.com**). However, before a designer can design a web site you will have to decide what you want your web site to do and what content you want to include. For more information on the importance of content see below.

When thinking about how you want your site to look beware of too much technical wizardry it is often distracting and one cautionary tale illustrates the possible dangers. A few years ago when the web site for Coleman Tilley Tarrant and Sutton (**http://www.ctts.co.uk**) was

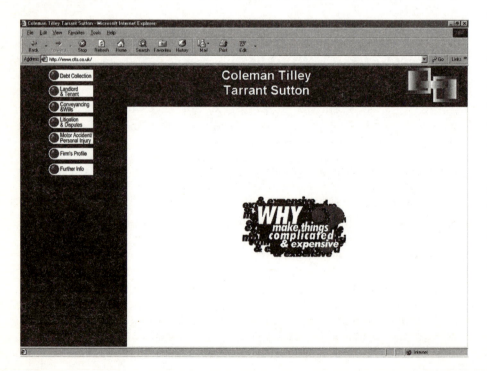

first set up the proposal was to have a banner reading "Why make things complicated and expensive?" In the initial version of the site the word "Why" was not in text but in graphics. This left a lot of visitors to the site, whose web browsers were not capable of reading the graphic left with the message: Coleman Tilley Tarrant and Sutton—make things complicated and expensive! As you can imagine the firm were not overjoyed and as the designers told me they had a "learning experience".

Web Sites

One of my favourites for sheer looks is the web site for Peter Carter Ruck and Partners (**http://www.carter-ruck.co.uk**). It is quick and simple, with clean, clear lines and carries through the identifiable brand from the paper marketing brochures. It also very clearly states the unique selling point of the firm—"we are defamation lawyers and we are the best at what we do". So many web sites fail to adequately show off the best points of the firm. The site also starts off with a "Welcome", giving you the feeling that you are entering part of the firm itself rather than a static brochure. Otherwise the site contains the information you need about the lawyers, areas of practice and some examples of recent work undertaken together with good contact information.

Another quite different but good site is the Memery Crystal site (**http://www.memery-crystal.co.uk**). The home page highlights Memery Crystal's involvement with a high profile commercial deal and their expertise as commercial lawyers. Information is given on the partners, the different departments in the firm and clear information on who to contact on what matter. Like all good sites it is quick, easy to navigate and interesting.

Showing how simple a web site can be and still be an effective marketing tool is the web site of sole practitioner, Jennifer Buckle (**http://www.jbuckle.co.uk**). Again it is quick, simple and clear with a good use of colour.

Content

As well as deciding what you want your web site to look like you need to consider the question of content. A few basics are absolutely essential. Starting with clear and easily found contact information. This should include the address, e-mail addresses and the telephone number of the firm. Another basic rule is to make sure that clear information is provided, like the firms areas of work. Is it purely an intellectual property firm or is it a general high street practice that can do your conveyancing? A visitor to the site needs to know this information and know it fast. Make sure it is immediately obvious what you do and what your skills are. The third essential category of information would be names and details of the fee earners working in the practice.

Once the basics are in place the actual content of the site is a matter of choice. The plan must be to make it as interesting as possible and hopefully to persuade people to stay on site for as long as possible. Giving you the chance of converting a visitor into a client.

One way to persuade people, or more accurately prospective clients, to hang around for a while seems to be to provide well directed educational material. For a general practice this is often a straight-forward explanation of how to get divorced or of a conveyancing transaction. For the more specialised practice this will be detailed legal information on a specific topic drawing in the industry professionals so that when they do have a legal problem they will think of the experts they are familiar with.

A good example of an educational site being used to attract clients in a specific industry would be DLA's (**http://www.dla.net**) subsite devoted to e-commerce. There is a lot of legal information on copyright, government policy, domain names, etc. No doubt, DLA hope that their site will become a regular port of call for those in the business, building trust and loyalty and gaining clients in the process. Some firms provide a similar service by e-mailing newsletters to their clients on relevant legal topics or providing an alert service when changes in the law occur.

Managing Your Web Site

It is rarely sufficient even for the simplest sites: to design it, put it up on the web and hope for the best. Web sites need managing.

It will therefore be necessary to employ a manager to ensure that the web site is kept up to date and in working order. Your web designer might undertake this function or be able to recommend a firm that specializes in this area.

Marketing Your Web Presence

Once you have a web site up and running, it is imperative that people know about it. This can involve making sure that the site is listed with all the search engines. This is usually done by the designer of the web site and can be a time consuming and frustrating business. But in reality people are not going to find your web site by surfing the Web.

I have set out below some simple rules to market a web site. One of these rules is to consider joining one of the online referral agencies and another is to ensure that a firm is listed in all necessary directories. I have therefore, after this section, set out details of online referral agencies and directories.

The Rules:

1. Make sure the firm's URL is on everything: brochures, business cards and notepaper.
2. In all advertisements ensure the URL is included.
3. Consider joining one of the online referral agencies (see below).
4. List your site with online and other directories including your URL.
5. Be the expert: if there is so much information on site that it is where the industry and journalists go, then potential clients will find out about it and journalists will write about it.
6. If your site is innovative it will get written about.
7. Research sites for relevant professional associations, see if your firm can advertise on site or more simply link to a relevant site.

Directories and Referral Services

One way of making your presence known on the Internet is by joining one of the referral services or by getting listed in an online directory. Referral services on the web appear to be mushrooming up everywhere and for the high street practice would appear to offer a potential source of new clients.

Referral Services

This must be one of the fastest growing legal services on the Internet.

Everywhere you look there is another site aiming to draw in the public. There are general sites and sites catering for specialties. For the right type of firms and if the right network is chosen at the right price, joining one of these schemes must be near the top of the list for the marketing budget.

The National Solicitors Network has managed to nab two of the best legal domain names for their referral site (**http://www.solicitor.co.uk** and **http://www.lawyer.co.uk**). The Internet presence builds on their name and offers another form of marketing for their panels of solicitors. Their promise to vet member firms for quality in the delivery of legal services gives a new client the reassurance that they are instructing a recommended firm rather than a completely unknown quantity.

LawNet (**http://www.lawnet.co.uk**) from Desktop Lawyer also promises to vet firms for quality before they are allowed to join the LawNet group. A potential client gives details on the area of work they need advice on and LawNet forwards the details to the nearest firm in the group. The client also has the option of contacting a member firm directly. The solicitor's firms benefiting from the added referrals and the clients from the assurance of quality.

Another product from Desktop Lawyer (**http://www.desktoplawyer. net**) is Direct Law. The DirectLaw service (**http://www.directlaw. co.uk**) is another type of referral service, this time all the firms on the database are subscribers to the Desktop Lawyer software and the promise you are getting is that the lawyer will be able to provide services online as well as standard legal services.

There are a lot of specialist referral sites which solicitors might consider joining, their names generally speak for themselves. These include Accident Compensation.com (**http://www.accidentcomp ensation.com**), Conveyancing Marketing Services (**http://www. conveyancing-cms.co.uk**) and Family Advice (**http://www.family advice.co.uk**).

Directories

Sweet and Maxwell give free access to the Kimes Directory on their site (**http://www.smlawpub.co.uk**). This is a searchable international law directory. It contains information on firms and chambers in over 250 countries. Each entry gives the names of the partners, languages spoken and work undertaken.

The Interactive-lawyer (**http://www.interactive-lawyer.com**) hosts Waterlows directory. This is a searchable directory of U.K. lawyers. A link is given to the firm by e-mail or to their web site.

The International Centre for Commercial Law (**http://www. icclaw.com**) is the official site of the Legal 500 on the web. The database contains firms in the U.K., Europe, Asia, USA and the Middle East. Firms are arranged in league tables for the different areas of their practice and a lot of information is given on recommended lawyers including their hobbies and where they went to school. A lot of contact information is given but there are no direct links.

There is also a searchable database of support services on file, including IT support, translators and recruitment consultants.

If you are looking for a specific firm of solicitors then the Delia Venables site (**http://www.venables.co.uk**) has an extensive listing of links. It is also worth a look at the Infolaw site (**http://www. infolaw.co.uk**).

Firms Offering Services Online

A lot of firms have started to offer legal services on the Internet. The sheer variety of approaches taken by the firms highlight how flexible the technology is and how important it is going to be for the future of all lawyers. This section is going to look at some examples of how firms are using the Internet to provide new services and how they are delivering old services in new ways. I have split this section up into two parts to look at the large city firms with their open ended budgets and a look at the smaller firms who in their own way are just as innovative.

Large City Firms

Looking first at the major city firms. The best known and the first off the starting block was Linklater's Blue Flag Service (**http:// www.linklaters.com/blueflag**). Blue Flag products are essentially "off the shelf" legal advice for complex legal situations. They are geared towards situations that while they do not require an individual lawyer to give individual advice do require expert legal knowledge. The advice is provided and tailored to the client's specific needs by the client answering a series of questions and proceeding down different paths towards the correct answer depending upon the responses given. The first product launched was Blue Flag Regulatory aimed at legal and compliance professionals working in investment and commercial banks, securities houses and fund management. This and the other four products provide advice 24 hours a day on the Internet, so your time zone does not restrain whether you can call your lawyer for advice or not. The advice is, of course, quicker and cheaper than the individual advice of a lawyer. The newest package offered by Blue Flag is Blue Flag Confirms, an application of similar technology to document production. Not surprisingly and probably the first of many Linklaters are now considering hiving off Blue Flag and expanding the concept away from strictly legal advice to more general commercial advice as well.

A different approach, but with the same basic principles as Blue Flag has been taken by S.J. Berwin (**http://www.sjberwin.com/media**). They have developed a product called the media wizard, available to clients on their web site. The media wizard takes a complex area of statutory law and regulation: cross media ownership and simplifies the process of solving a client's queries. A scenario of ownership is fed into the wizard. The wizard digests the information and responds by highlighting potential conflicts and problems. A service a media lawyer could easily provide given more time and at a greater cost.

Berwin Leighton (**http://www.berwinleighton.com**) have gone down the independent road from the start with the creation of their e-commerce product, Be-Professional. This independent venture created in partnership with Deloitte & Touche will provide online business solutions to small and medium sized enterprises. By starting an e-commerce business from scratch Berwin Leighton appear to be expanding the role of the legal partnership away from that of a simple provider of legal services into a more entrepreneurial one.

Allen and Overy (**http://www.allenovery.com**) have taken a different approach to using the Internet in their business and one that would appear to be a model that a lot of other firms are already or are considering adopting for the future. It is an obvious example of the benefits of Internet technology over paper. The Allen and Overy Internet based product is called newchange dealroom. The newchange dealroom is a secure ring fenced area of the Internet set aside for collecting together all the documents and information on a transaction in one place. The idea is that every commercial transaction managed by Allen and Overy will have its own secure newchange dealroom web site with all the documentation, contacts and deal information on site. Access to this web site or part of it will be restricted to authorised users. Allen and Overy will control the site and will post documents on to the site, when these have been posted relevant persons will be notified by e-mail and they will be able to access the site or the relevant part of it for their needs. Documents will be able to be downloaded and amendments to documents made. All the documentation for one deal will be in one place accessible by all necessary parties at all times. No more biking bulky documents across London or shipping to Hong Kong for 9 a.m.

The same basic idea has been used by Clifford Chance (**http://www.cliffordchance.com**) in its Fruit Net virtual dealroom. Fruit Net was developed for a specific deal and was used for the rapid distribution of documents, as a centralised storage facility and also contained searchable information on 115 target companies. Clifford Chance proposes to expand the concept of Fruit Net to more multi-party and multi-jurisdictional transactions.

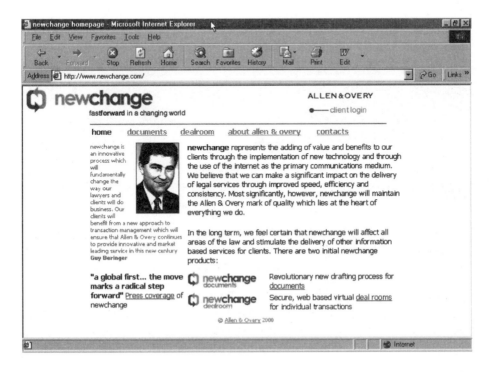

Small Firms

The smaller firms have not been outdone in their use of technology. Kaye Tesler and Company (**http://www.kt.uklegal.net**) were one of the first to provide legal services on the Internet. They now provide an extensive list of services from interactive form filling for wills to quotes and initial instructions for conveyancing. They also give initial advice on litigation matters and some company and commercial matters online. Kaye Tesler is obviously not sitting on its technological laurels as it is in the process of setting up video conferencing facilities for its clients, taking the travel out of meetings: saving clients time and money.

Another early entrant in the Internet stakes was Fidler and Pepper (**http://www.fidler.co.uk**). On their bold and bright site aimed squarely at the general public they offer online services and online matter reporting enabling you to check the progress on your case anytime of the day or night. Fidler and Pepper expect 10 per cent of their business to come from the web by the end of 2000 and have imaginative expansion plans for their web based services. These include providing low cost commoditised legal advice programs aimed

at the general public. There will also be a more advanced package enabling clients to run their own simple case online. Telephone back up and customised legal advice for the more complex transactions will be available as well.

Bevan and Co (**http://www.bevans.co.uk**) have a young fresh looking web site. They provide quite a lot of online services and offer free initial advice online and free standard documentation online.

Berwin Bloomer's web site (**http://www.berwin.co.uk**) is attractive, quick and easy to get around. Berwin Bloomer appear to be just starting on the road from purely marketing their firm with their impressive web site to providing online legal services. At the moment services offered are simple conveyancing quotes and the taking of instructions online. But as a new partner in Desktop Lawyer's Direct Law network Berwin Bloomer is set to offer an extensive range of legal documents online. Plans are also underway to provide clients with online access to progress reports on their files.

An Internet Firm?

Definitely not easily categorized, FirstLaw has been billed as the first Internet law firm (**http://www.firstlaw.co.uk**). FirstLaw is not a law firm in the traditional sense. What FirstLaw does is to act as a broker between clients and law firms. Clients post work onto the FirstLaw site. This piece of work is then put out to tender to qualified law firms who then make sealed bids for the work. The service opens up solicitor's fees to commercial pressure and gives clients some bargaining power for the first time. Even given this, a lot of established commercial firms have signed up. It seems that FirstLaw has been of particular interest to commercial firms outside London. These firms can be competitive on price while gaining access to clients they would not necessarily have been able to attract otherwise.

CHAPTER FIVE

CHAMBERS AND BARRISTERS

There is a strange dichotomy between the ancient traditions and approach of some of the institutions of the Bar and the activities and enthusiasm of some individual barristers for the new technology. Some Chambers (not all by any means) realise how the Internet can be used to raise their profile, to attract more solicitors and other professional clients and to cheaply and successfully market worldwide to overseas clients who can, of course, instruct them direct.

In this section I am going to attempt to cover all the different aspects of the Bar on the web including the organisations that govern and make up the Bar, services for barristers online and the best chambers web sites. I will conclude by looking at some of the sites of individual barristers who in the best traditions of the Bar have been some of the great innovators when it comes to seeing the potential of law on the Internet.

Associations

The Bar Council (http://www.barcouncil.org.uk)

The Bar Council site sets the tone for a lot of the Bar sites with a lengthy discourse on the history and the role of the Bar. Luckily unlike some other sites it doesn't stop there. The notice board in particular contains a wealth of information on legal developments affecting the Bar with the majority of documents available for reading on site or downloadable in pdf (see p. 58). You will find information on the Woolf Reforms, Community Legal Service and a paper comparing the economic cost of barristers to solicitors among others. While if you were thinking about training to become a barrister the information on site in the education and training section would be essential reading, especially the statistics on the numbers of graduates from the BVC and the number of pupillages available. There is also a well used discussion forum with questions from students, pupils and barristers.

The Criminal Bar Association (http://www.criminalbar.com)

The Criminal Bar Association site is a simple site for members of the association. Facilities include the CBA Newsletter, Archbold News and Current Sentencing Practice News. There are also a good set of links on site, in particular, a long list of university law departments.

The Commercial Bar Association (http://www.combar.com)

The Commercial Bar Association site is limited to history on the role of the Bar and contact details for members, chambers and barristers.

The Inns of Court

Grays Inn: (**http://www.graysinn.org.uk**)

Inner Temple: (**http://www.innertemple.org.uk**)

Lincoln's Inn: (**http://www.lincolnsinn.org.uk**)

Middle Temple: (**http://www.middletemple.org.uk**)

Having looked at all the web sites for the Inns of Court it is even more difficult to work out their function than before. The web sites focus strongly on the historical with a lot of information on the history and the role of the Bar. There is interesting information on the historical buildings within the Inns. The impression given by the web sites is of a group looking back into history. One noteworthy feature on most of the sites is the details of the quite spectacular function rooms available to hire.

The Bar Pro Bono Unit (http://www.barprobono.org.uk)

The Pro Bono Unit site is there to publicise the work of the unit, to solicitors and clients and to raise money.

Services for the Bar Online

Portals

The first dedicated portal for barristers is now online (**http://www.redbag.co.uk**). Redbag is very much a newcomer and at the time of writing a lot of the promised services are still under construction. These services include chambers and barristers directories, legal links, reviews of useful web sites, a special section for juniors and templates of pleadings and other documentation. One particular feature will be a search engine that allows solicitors and others to find barristers, a service in competition with the Lawyers Online and Book Counsel services. Given the small number of barristers in total in the U.K. it will be interesting to see if any other competitors come into the market or whether potential competitors presume that the general legal portals and communities will appeal equally to barristers and solicitors.

Booking Services

Another new development is the ability to book counsel online. There are, apart from the Redbag service, two contenders at the moment. Book Counsel's (**http://www.bookcounsel.com**) aim is to "enervate and release the potential of the young Bar". Book Counsel is independent, privately financed and at the moment free to all users. Within a month of launch Book Counsel was getting 1,600 hits per day, even given the fact that 95 per cent of visitors to the site are browsers, they still must be onto something. The same stable is also launching a site for the online booking of expert witnesses (**http://www.bookwitnesses.com**).

The Lawyers Online service (**http://www.lawyersonline.co.uk**) is rather different. Again the essence of the service is to enable the booking of counsel online. The catch, for the barristers, with the Lawyers Online service is that the intention is to create a market with the barristers clerks tendering for the proposed work and the winner being the lowest tender for the best quality barrister.

Bar Directories

There are a lot of ways to find a barrister. One way is to use the Bar Directories, one of the best known is the Sweet and Maxwell directory (**http://www.sweetandmaxwell.co.uk/bar/index**). This directory gives an index of barristers and chambers searchable by name, region or

175

speciality. Another way to find a barrister would be to use the International Centre for Commercial Law, Legal 500 service (**http://www.icclaw.com**). The Legal 500 recommends barristers and chambers in different fields of law. The top seniors and juniors are ranked in tables together with a commentary on the top performers in different cases. Finally, a lot of legal portals have a site where barristers or chambers can register their web details. Try Delia Venables website (**http://www.venables.co.uk**) or once it is up and running, Redbag (**http://www.redbag.co.uk**).

Chambers

Unlike a lot of other sites connected with the Bar some of the chambers sites portray a very modern, technologically advanced image. On the best sites time is not wasted going over the history of the Bar, but concentrated more on what these sets have to offer in the future.

One of my favourites is the Hardwicke Building site (**http://www.hardwicke.co.uk**). It is up to date, clear, accessible and quick. If you have Flash software a short presentation can be viewed with lots of zooming red words. If you don't, Flash can be downloaded off the site or the presentation can be watched without the graphic effects. Whatever you do it is not an essential part of the site, more a bit of fun. The Property Law Group at Hardwicke Building has an impressive sub site with news, articles and case commentaries. A useful resource for any property solicitors and no doubt an effective marketing tool when it comes down to solicitors deciding who they are going to instruct. The site as a whole gives the impression of a very modern pro-active group of lawyers.

The Doughty Street Chambers site (**http://www.doughtystreet.co.uk**) uses colour to good effect and again makes the chambers appear modern and progressive. The contact information is excellent and really accessible. For those interested in human rights law there are news, views and articles on site to keep the practitioner up to date with developments together with an excellent set of human rights links.

2 Temple Gardens (**http://www.2templegardens.co.uk**) doesn't look that great but it was one of the first to provide a real service to the legal profession with its commentary on the Woolf Reforms. The commentary is still available and is a simple, easily digestible explanation of the effects of the new civil procedure rules.

Another one to watch is Design Chambers (**http://www. designchambers.com**). The web site doesn't have bells and whistles like a lot of other chambers' sites but it is quick and effective at conveying the message. The chambers is a small set active in the fields of e-commerce, media and intellectual property and given the areas of interest it is no surprise that they are one of the sets best equipped to take advantage of the new technology. At present as barristers are barred from taking direct instructions any received are passed on to a panel of media and I.P. practices. But the set is well poised to take advantage of any loosening of the regulations controlling access to the Bar and would be the first in the queue to offer specialized legal advice over the Internet. This is definitely one to watch, it will be interesting to see what they do next.

A couple of other attractive, informative and easy to navigate sites are those for Blackstone Chambers (**http://www.blackstone.co.uk**) and Fountain Court (**http://www.fountaincourt.co.uk**).

Individual Barrister Sites

Some barristers have grasped the meaning of the new technology faster than any other lawyers. In particular, some barristers stand out for having realised the potential of the Internet to inform, educate and pontificate way before the rest of us had even woken up. I am going to mention a few notables but there are others and more joining in by the day.

Laurie West-Knight is one of the great enthusiasts for the potential of Internet technology. A newly made up Queen's Counsel barrister at 4 Paper Buildings and the Vice Chair of the Society for Computers and Law, he is one of the driving forces behind the Bailii Project which is aiming to put U.K. law on the Internet, freely accessible and hyperlinked. His own website (**http://www.lawonline.cc**) contains a lot more information on Bailii as well as its precursor the Australian, AustLII. The main focus of the site though is the commentary on the civil procedure rules. This can only be accessed with a password, but these are freely available.

Roger Horne is another of the barristers who has had a site on the Internet for some time. His site called Roger Horne's Miscellany (**http://www.hrothgar.co.uk**) is just that. It is a mixture of papers by Mr Horne on a variety of legal issues. There is also links to Roger Horne's civil procedure rules site, YAWS.

Gary Webber's site (**http://www.garywebber.co.uk**) is aimed at property lawyers and surveyors. It is essentially an attractive advertisement for the services of Gary Webber, the barrister. It contains information for property lawyers on property and the civil procedure rules and boundary disputes.

A similar site in effect is the site by barrister Neil Addison and solicitor-advocate Timothy Lawson-Crittenden. Their site, Harassment Law U.K. (**http://www.harassment-law.co.uk**) provides detailed information to the public and other lawyers on the relatively new area of harassment law. In doing this they are setting out their stall as the experts in this area of law and hoping to attract clients and referrals on this basis.

CHAPTER SIX

CAREERS IN THE LAW ONLINE

It is not only possible to research and plan a legal career on the web it is essential to do so. University, firm and chambers web sites provide far more information than a simple brochure and in making career decisions information is the essential factor. Universities and colleges expect you to have browsed their site and to have downloaded application forms and prospectuses. Firms do not expect to be asked questions in interviews on matters that are published on their web site. The general expectation whether you are applying to study or to a firm or chambers is that you will have done your research and the primary focus of that research is going to be relevant web sites.

This section is going to take you through a career in the law from the initial decision to become a lawyer, to university, the LPC or BVC and on into work. The last part is on continuing professional development online. It should therefore be easy to pick up the thread at the appropriate place for your career.

Careers Sites

Starting at the beginning it may be the case that you are reading this before you have definitely decided that you want a career in the law. If this is the case then there are several general career sites that will provide you with information and links on any career that interests you. Career Zone (**http://www.careerzone-uk.com**) is one, as well as providing links on legal careers there is also advice on interview techniques and the writing of curriculum vitaes.

Once the decision has been made to pursue a career in the law it is necessary to find out about the relevant options. Do you want to qualify as a barrister or a solicitor? What are the different routes to qualification? The most useful web sites in this area are those run by the professions governing bodies. The Law Society site (**http://**

www.lawsociety.org.uk) has a section devoted to qualifying as a solicitor, providing detailed information on the different routes to qualification, qualifying law degrees, the legal practice course and training contracts. There is also provision on site to contact the Law Society with any further queries. The General Council of the Bar (**http://www.barcouncil.org.uk**) has a similar section on education and training providing the essential information for anyone considering a career at the Bar. Another useful resource is the Law Careers Advice Network (**http://www.prospects.csu.man.ac.uk/student/cidd/lcan/main.htm**). This site is intended for careers advisers but it is equally informative for anyone considering a legal career. As well as information on legal careers and links to the Law Society and Bar sites, it also offers figures on the range of careers taken up by law graduates and the shortage of places for pupillage.

Universities

Having decided to take the next step to study for a degree or maybe considering further legal study, whichever it is, it will be necessary to research the relevant universities. The easiest way to find a university law school is by using the comprehensive set of links at the National Centre for Legal Education (**http://www.warwick.ac.uk/ncle**). Follow the links from "Teaching and Learning Resources" to "Institutions offering Law Courses". If the university you are looking for is not listed it is usually quite simple to guess the URL as it will generally specify the city or college name and end in **ac.uk**. Sometimes an accepted abbreviation for the city or college will be used instead.

The majority of law school web pages are very similar in content. You will find information about the university and the city and detailed information on undergraduate and postgraduate law degrees, courses, research projects and specialised centres at the university, together with contact names and addresses.

Legal Practice Course

A lot of institutions are validated by the Law Society to offer the Legal Practice Course. Although, all the providers are listed in the Law Society pages there are no URLs or links. The easiest way to research all the different institutions is to start off at the Central Applications Board site (**http://www.lawcabs.ac.uk**). The Central Application Board processes all applications for the Legal Practice

Course, Common Professional Examination or Post Graduate Diploma in Law at whatever institution it is to be taken. The site also has a list of all institutions offering the courses and links to pages detailing the fees, size and other issues for the relevant course. There is also, importantly, a link to the web site of the law school in question. It is not possible to apply to the Central Applications Board online but you can register your interest and an application pack will be sent to you. Looking at a couple of the major provider's sites:

The College of Law (**http://www.lawcol.org.uk**) site sets out all the information you could need on the Legal Practice Course and all the other legal activities that the College is involved in. The College is also using the Internet in the provision of services, in a simple way by enabling a prospective student to order a prospectus online or to book a place at an open day. In a more complex way the College is using the Internet for its current students by allowing access to restricted areas of the site for students to download course material or to take advantage of careers advice. In the natural progression of things the College will no doubt be offering a legal qualification obtained online in the next couple of years.

BPP Law School site was, unfortunately, at the time of writing under construction. All that was available was a very small amount of information on BPP's general site (**http://www.bpp.co.uk**).

The Cardiff Law School Site (**http://www.cardiff.ac.uk/claws**) is probably the most impressive to look at. It is also quick and easy to get around and contains all the information you could want to know about the LPC at Cardiff.

Similarly, the Nottingham Law School site (**http://www.nls.ntu.ac.uk**) is packed with information on the legal programs offered at Nottingham.

The Oxford Institute of Legal Practice (**http://www.oxilp.ac.uk**) is another well-respected institution offering the LPC. The web site is very similar in appearance, functionality and content to a lot of others but the URL is not to be found in the usual places so to make life simpler it is stated above.

Bar Vocational Course

The Bar Vocational Course is offered currently by the following institutions:

Inns of Court School of Law	(**http://www.icsl.ac.uk**)
College of Law	(**http://www.lawcol.org.uk**)
BPP Law School	(**http://www.bpp.co.uk**)
University of Northumbria	(**http://www.unn.ac.uk**)
Cardiff Law School jointly	(**http://www.cardiff.ac.uk/claws**
and with the University of the	(**http://www.uwe.ac.uk**)
West of England	
Manchester Metropolitan University	(**http://www.mmu.ac.uk**)
Nottingham Law School	(**http://www.nls.ntu.ac.uk**)

All the above also offer the legal practice course, the Inns of Court School of Law being a new entrant in this field. The majority of the sites give all the information needed. The Inns of Court School of Law site is particularly good, easy to navigate and quick.

All applications for the Bar vocational course are handled by the Central Applications Clearing House (CACH). This is dealt with by the General Council of the Bar (**http://www.barcouncil.org.uk**). It is not possible to apply or register online but relevant contact details are provided.

The Institute of Legal Executives

It should never be forgotten that there are other careers in the law. The Institute of Legal Executives (**http://www.ilex.org.uk**) site must be an indispensable resource to anyone considering a career as a legal executive. The site contains a lot of detailed information on the requirements to train as a legal executive, courses to be taken, exams to be passed and Law Society Regulations.

The Training Contract

With the advent of the Internet and firm's web sites it is so much easier to research firms to apply to. It is no longer a question of trying to find the right brochures in the careers room or sending off for a brochure to 10 possibilities. Now it is possible to look at a whole range of different firms, get an idea of the type of work they do, the culture and size of the firm, overseas opportunities and their attitude to the use of technology in the delivery of legal services. Surprisingly, not that many firms provide an area of their web site specifically for applicants for training contracts. It would seem a simple enough thing to do and a good marketing exercise. Of those that do, Addleshaw Booth and Company is one of the best (**http://www.addleshaw-booth.co.uk**) with trainee testimonials, a trainee chat messaging forum and the ability to download an application form on site. Allen and Overy (**http://www.allenovery.com**) and Norton Rose (**http://www.nortonrose.com**) have good areas devoted to potential trainees.

Pupillage

It is now much easier to find out about the different chambers and the different Inns. All the Inns have web sites and the majority of chambers do as well. Like solicitor's firms it is a question of doing your research. Check out as many sites as possible read about the different areas of law, the careers of the different barristers, noteworthy cases undertaken, IT resources of chambers and the training for pupils.

The majority of applications for pupillage are handled by the Bar Council's Pupillage Application Clearing House (PACH). Details of this can be found on the Bar Council site in the education and training section, but it is not possible to register your interest or to apply via the web site online. This is strange as all applications for PACH have to be submitted in electronic form.

Some chambers have chosen not to take part in the PACH scheme. For these chambers it is still necessary to apply directly to them. Chambers' web sites will specify what form of application is acceptable. To find a list of all the chambers, their areas of work, size, make-up and policy on applications it is necessary to purchase a copy of the The Bar Council's Chambers, Pupillages and Awards Handbook available in all law libraries or from the Bar Council.

Post Qualification Employment

Virtually all qualified solicitors posts are advertised in online legal news magazines or are handled through recruitment consultancies, again virtually all of which can be browsed online. Barristers to date have been less mobile, probably because they are self-employed and compared to solicitors there are not that many of them. On one or two chambers' sites applications for new tenants are welcomed, but there is not, as yet, a large market in the employment of barristers. So, having said that, this section will focus on jobs for solicitors or barristers in private practice.

Interactive Lawyer (**http://www.interactive-lawyer.com**) has a job search area where you can enter criteria for any post and a search will be made on your behalf to find jobs that match your criteria. If a suitable job is found it is possible to e-mail your interest on a contact form and to paste your CV to this. The Interactive Lawyer has incorporated what used to be known as The Lawyer Online into their site, so the jobs database is essentially the same as for the hard copy of The Lawyer.

The Interactive Lawyer also has a recruitment consultants register. This lists a large number of legal recruitment consultants with further information and hyperlinks to a few of the larger ones. As a way of finding the consultancies operating in your area it is very useful.

The Law Society Gazette (**http://www.lawgazette.co.uk**) offers two services. The job search is very similar in set up to the Interactive Lawyer job search. You enter your criteria for a job and a search is made of the jobs database, matching jobs are then posted on screen. The second service is the job tracker. This is a more interactive way of finding a job and fits in well with the newly customisable online Gazette. To use this service you need to specify your job criteria on a form, then whenever a job comes up that matches your criteria an e-mail will be sent to notify you.

Recruitment Consultants

A couple of the recruitment sites that do not have links on the Interactive Lawyer site at the moment are worth mentioning. Firstly, the Zarak Group site (**http://www.zarakgroup.com/zmb/ private_practice**) this has useful comparative information on salaries and lawyer's experiences in different work environments as well as advice on how to draft a CV and to perform at an interview. The Chambers and Partners site (**http://www.chambersandpartners. com**) offers an opportunity to buy the Chambers Directories as well as recruitment contact information. The Charles Fellowes Partnership is not yet online, though plans are well underway (**http:// www.charlesfellowes.com**). The surprising factor about all these sites and the majority of other recruitment consultancy sites is how basic they are, very few put jobs online and those that do often have a registration requirement before you are allowed to browse. The recruitment business is very obviously a people business and it will never be possible to recruit a solicitor solely online, but more use could be made of the possibilities of the Internet to entice in the best clients and lawyers.

Continuing Professional Development

All solicitors are required to complete a certain number of hours per year of further legal education. This will be a requirement for barristers as well in the near future. Currently most CPD hours are achieved by attending lectures and seminars away from the office, by watching LNTV videos and by attending internal training sessions run by a firms' training department. A new method of delivery has recently entered the market with online CPD. This is currently offered by a few providers like Lawyers Online and I believe that The College of Law intends to enter this market.

The opportunities that online CPD can offer are only just being realised. The Internet offers the convenience of being available 24 hours a day and being accessible from anywhere. Already online video presentations and real time tutorials and seminars are offered. While both have their place they do not really take advantage of the ability of the Internet to be able to host interactive programs.

It will be interesting to see what online CPD products are developed and whether any really grasp the fact that learning could actually be made to be fun if sufficient imagination was invested. Some firms and chambers have already added an education function to their role, with lectures and seminars given to the wider legal audience. Maybe given that the function of firms is changing, with the floating off of Internet products and the creation of separate legal entities to manage Internet driven businesses, some firm will create a training division that actually makes money through the development of an unrivalled online CPD program.

Are You Ready for the Web?

Having read the whole of the section on the Best of the Rest can you now say that you are ready:

- Do you read all your legal news online?

- Have you customised your online Gazette yet?

- Have you created your own mini portal by collecting together your favourite sites on your bookmark or setting up your portal with My Findlaw?

- Do you check out online recruiters whenever you look at the Interactive Lawyer?

- Have you contributed to an online legal discussion yet?

- Are all legal forms used downloaded from the Internet?

- Have you checked out your future employer's site yet? Do you still want to work for them?

Part D: Where Do We Go From Here?

CHAPTER ONE

E-COMMERCE FOR LAWYERS

What are the Opportunities?

One of the first questions that needs asking is what exactly is meant by the term "e-commerce". One definition from ecentreUK defines e-commerce as "any form of business or administrative transaction or information exchange that is executed using any information and communications technology, this embraces business to business; business to consumer; and government to nation; as well as exchange tools like the Internet and the world wide web, Intranets, Extranets, e-mail and electronic data interchange (EDI)". This definition would include the use of: e-mail, subscription research services like Lawtel and Westlaw, surfing the Web, using an office Intranet and practice and case management systems. Applying this definition (hopefully) every lawyer in the country is involved in e-commerce to some extent. While ecentreUK's definition defines the broad range of activities that can constitute e-commerce, I am going to focus on a narrower definition, namely: the use of the Internet and associated technology to facilitate the provision of legal services. Using this as the starting point I am going to attempt to set out some of the many ways that the Internet can be used in legal practices and chambers to improve the delivery of legal services to clients and to change and improve the management and profitability of law firms.

It has to be remembered and reinforced that the new economy is not just about IT firms and dotcoms; it includes every legal practice in the country and given this fact lawyers need to learn to think in new ways to fit the new order. Everything is changing and changing fast and those that can't or don't want to keep up will be left behind. As Joe Reevy, editor of online legal community LawZone says, "firms have to realise that they don't need to invest in IT to make more money, but to stay in business". With one million new users of the Internet in the first six months of 2000 it is not going to be long before the majority of the population are Internet literate and expect services to be available online. It would be a shame if the few left out included lawyers with their heads in the sand.

Grant Thornton, a business and financial consultancy firm conducted a survey on IT use in law firms, The Legal IT Interfirm Comparison. The results make interesting reading. While 59 per cent of firms have their own web site, this figure hides the disparities between the 92 per cent of large firms that have a web site and the much lower 48 per cent of firms with 10 partners or less who do. This figure should make frightening reading for senior partners in small firms. If any sector of the legal market needs to take advantage of the potential of the Web to increase their workload and turnover then it must be the small high street practice, seeing its client base being attacked from all sides. Whether it is from franchising, online conveyancing or the might of Desktop Lawyer it must be getting harder to meet targets everyday. These bare figures of uptake on web sites also fail to highlight how little the majority of firms are doing with their web presence. Having trawled the nether reaches of the web for legal web sites I can only agree with Grant Thorntons' findings that the majority of firms are not using their web sites to their full potential. There are a large number of unattractive, slow and dull sites around and this is not even considering the issue of whether the firms are using their web presence to provide services online. Surprisingly, the survey found that no large firms that responded to the survey carried out any legal transactions on the Web, while 22.4 per cent of the smaller firms had either received instructions or given quotes via their web site. It could be argued that the type of business undertaken by the larger firms does not lend itself to taking instructions online or the giving of online quotes. Though the success of the new Internet law firm, FirstLaw, would not seem to back this up.

While on the one hand it might make bleak reading that only just over half of all firms have a web site and few firms make use of technology to provide services online. On the other hand it also advertises the fact that the field is still wide open to any firm that really wants to make a difference to their practice by using new technology. In thinking about what opportunities are available firms and lawyers need to consider four basic issues:

1. How can you use the Internet to improve services to clients?

2. Can you use the Internet to provide new services for clients and to attract more clients?

3. Should a firm create a separate business to develop and market Internet services?

4. How can you use the Internet to improve the management of your business?

Taking these issues in turn:

1. How can you Use the Internet to Improve Services to Clients?

E-mail

E-mail is so common that it is often forgotten that it is a creature of the Internet. Nearly every legal practice is familiar with e-mail and a lot of practices rely on e-mail for communication with the majority of their clients. But e-mail is not always as much of a boon as it should be. The whole point about e-mail is that it is fast. It is not fast if the time it takes to respond to it is as slow as to the average letter. If clients send information by e-mail they expect a response by e-mail and a quick one. It should be firm policy that all e-mails are responded to within two hours, if only by an acknowledgement that the matter is being investigated. In order to facilitate this quick response to e-mails all the rest of the junk that clutters up ones e-mail must be controlled or lawyers will suffer from information overload. The installation of appropriate software to keep out junk mail, separate e-mail accounts for internal memoranda, policies on: copying the whole firm inappropriately, using alternatives like the telephone or voice mail and the filtering of e-mails through a secretary are all part of the solution. Encryption should also be considered where appropriate. E-mail is also useful for the distribution of newsletters to clients to keep them abreast of the latest developments and nowadays all part of the service expected from a firm.

Legal Research

Another simple method by which the Internet can improve the service offered to existing clients is by using the legal research products to keep lawyers up to date in their areas of speciality. Given the availability of some excellent Internet research tools a lawyer should always be well informed on the latest cases, opinions and statutory developments. For too long a lot of smaller practices have had poor, often out of date, library resources mainly because of the high cost of books, staffing and space in providing a full library. There are no longer any excuses. Sole practitioner Matthew Boyer, an expert charities and environmental lawyer considers the 20 page e-mail he gets daily from Lawtel to be a very important part of his practice. The information provided by Lawtel is tailored to his areas of expertise and ensures that he is as up to date as any solicitor in a large practice with libraries and know-how lawyers.

According to the Grant Thornton survey it is still the case that more firms rely on paper based research resources than the Internet. This is a staggering fact given the research resources available and the relative cheapness of Internet research products compared to the maintainence and staffing of a library. A lot of firms do use CD-ROMs which although an improvement on a paper library still don't provide the breadth of the research possibilities available on the Internet.

Virtual Dealrooms

A simple innovation that is of great benefit to clients is the Allen and Overy virtual dealroom, newchange. By providing a ring fenced area on the Internet where all the documents and information for a deal can be stored, inspected, downloaded or amended, newchange is the sort of product that can make a real difference to the service provided to a client. It is only a matter of time before other firms are using the same idea as a standard way of doing business. Media firms will collect copy for libel reading from their virtual library and put it back when finished for the client to collect and multi-party litigations will have virtual case rooms where all the case files are stored.

Extranets

The use of secure extranets to link a major client into a firms system should also be considered. An Extranet makes it easy for a client to access their files online, to check the progress on different transactions and check out the current billing status. An Extranet can also help the exchange of information between lawyer and client. A client can simply and securely make available to their lawyers detailed information on their business and lawyers can keep clients well informed on the latest legal developments. The creation of an Extranet can help create client loyalty, the added investment by the firm showing the firms commitment to this client relationship.

Video Conferencing

One innovation that has been heralded for a long time but is only now becoming a reality is the introduction of video conferencing. It cuts down on travel costs of clients (and lawyers) and saves everybody's time. The prospect of screens built into the walls of a firms' conference room and the use of life size pictures rather than fuzzy faces in a computer monitor will be commonplace in a few years time. Investigating the potential of video conferencing should be on a lot of lawyers' lists.

Online Support

One possible way in which the current service given to clients could be improved by using the Internet is by offering online support. A lot of the time a client has a straightforward legal question that needs answering now. The client may be worried about being able to get hold of the right person to answer their query or of the cost involved. A first port of call in this situation could be the lawyers' in-house online support team who might be able to provide the answer themselves or easily access someone who does and get back to the client within minutes online.

2. How can you Use the Internet to Provide New Services for Clients and to Attract More Clients?

In considering this question it is important to understand what the Internet and the technology associated with it is best at. The Internet is good at providing standard services like banking, watch the success of the Internet banks like Egg and Smile and the rush for all the other banks to offer their own Internet bank. The Internet is not good at selling designer sports clothes, note the collapse of **BOO.com**. There are too many variables in the buying of designer clothes, too many choices involved. Given this it is hardly surprising that the same issues arise in the provision of legal services online, the buzzwords in legal circles being commoditised and customised legal services. The commoditisation of legal services accepts the fact that a lot of what a lawyer does is routine. It comes as no surprise to most that one domestic conveyance follows very much the same process as the next and that unless you fall into the tax arrangement bracket a will is pretty standard stuff. For these and other essentially simple, repetitive transactions the Internet provides access to the interactive technology that provides the client with a quicker, cheaper and probably more responsive service. Commoditisation also accepts that the client is an intelligent human being capable of making rational choices about their legal needs. But the commoditisation of legal services does not stop at the simple domestic conveyance. Linklaters' Blue Flag service and S.J. Berwins' Media Wizard show that even when it appears to the outsider that complex questions of fact and law are involved, it is not always the case. Even what seems to be complex areas of law to the uninitiated, can be commoditised if the range of variables involved is not too broad. If a legal service can be commoditised then it can be sold to current clients and new clients over the Internet.

Given that the majority of services being provided over the Internet are going to be commoditised services, what type of services will these be? This question is next to impossible to answer as it is purely dependent on imagination and the speed at which technology advances. Even with services like online wills and conveyancing, there is a lot more development to come, whether in new software, a different spin on how services are delivered or even the scale and ambition behind the facade of a small high street firm.

> Fidler and Pepper were a small general practice essentially driven into the provision of online services by a depressed local economy and the realisation that new technology could offer opportunities to reach clients outside their immediate area.
> Offering a highly commoditised product Fidler and Pepper don't have to stop at being a small practice with a small web site. Property is cheap in Nottinghamshire and there is no reason why in a couple of years Fidler and Pepper shouldn't have a whole barn full of technology, lawyers and support staff providing conveyancing, wills, debt collection and other online services for the whole country. It is probably not how the current crop of undergraduates imagined their legal career developing, but for some it will be their working life if not with Fidler and Pepper then with someone else.

Some ideas currently out there include online employment law, using interactive questionnaires the initial promise of a case being assessed online.

3. Should a Firm Create a Separate Business to Develop and Market Internet Services?

Fidler and Pepper and a lot of the other online high street practices stick with their partnership identity for their online brand. For a lot of commercial firms, online services have been set up under a different name and branding either to distinguish low value commoditised services from the high value bricks and mortar practice or to project a modern fresh image.

Addleshaw Booth and Company's have set up a separate division called enact-online (**http://www.enact-online.co.uk**). The thinking behind this move was the perceived difficulties in attaching the new ways and ideas of working to an old-fashioned name like Addleshaw Booth. Enact-online provides fast and efficient online volume legal services for conveyancing and remortgaging to financial and corporate institutions. A major consultation was undertaken with clients before the product was launched ensuring that the service fitted their clients needs. New separate premises were also purchased and fitted out. But before enact could go online it was necessary to rethink how they conducted their business. It was realised that old methods and ways of thinking just wouldn't work online, forms were simplified, processes streamlined and then the move online was made. The service is currently newly operational, developments planned for the next few months include connecting clients to enact-online by secure Extranets and the ability for clients to view their own files online. Anthony Ruane, a partner with Addleshaw Booth and Company and the driving force behind enact-online, explained their ambition to become a centre of national excellence in their industry. He emphasised the need to come up with new ideas and products to ensure that enact stays ahead of the competition and attracts more and more clients.

Berwin Leighton by calling their product Be-Professional are, like Addleshaw and Booth, separating the Internet brand from their core business. In the case of Berwin Leighton this is further emphasised by their creating an independent company for the launch of their Internet product.

Linklaters are taking a similar route with the proposed spin off of Blue Flag.

The creation of independent companies to own and market Internet brands breaks new ground and raises questions about the changing role of a law firm in the Internet age.

It could be argued that the renaming of Dibb Lupton Alsopp as DLA is one way of making a partnership of the Internet age. Rather than creating a separate brand to market the Internet driven part of the business and calling it DLA; changing the name of the whole firm says that all of the business is modern and forward looking, removing the need to create a separate vehicle for Internet projects.

4. How can you Use the Internet to Improve the Management of your Business?

Thankfully not every legal service can be commoditised. Where there are complex facts to be teased apart, complex legal questions to be analysed and applied or the need to think and respond on one's feet; then the mind and training of a lawyer will always be needed. This being the case the idea of a law firm with offices where a client can go to seek legal advice will continue.

The most valuable members of any firm are the fee earners. Their earnings pay the costs of maintaining an office and the wages of the support staff. It is a simple fact that the earnings of the firm will be higher if the associated costs are reduced and the efficient working of the firm is not compromised.

The use of the Internet and associated technology in the working of a firm should be able to cut costs and improve the efficiency of the business.

Starting with a few simple steps that could be taken:

1. Use the Internet to purchase office supplies and IT equipment. E-Procurement can save costs by cutting out the paper bound bureaucracy in conventional ordering systems. A secure link can be set up with the supplier and standard ordering could be automated. Alternatively, the firm could use the Internet to access the market place and invite tenders for the supply of office or IT equipment.

2. Admit that the paper law library is redundant. The librarian would remain on board as a highly trained IT professional who can find the answer to any legal query, choose legal research products and

arrange the extensive training that all fee earners will need. But the actual physical presence of a library is done away with cutting costs for support staff, accommodation and books.

3. Do away with know-how lawyers. Only recently invented, the know-how lawyer is another casualty of the knowledge management revolution. Why would a firm need know-how lawyers? With a really good legal research product that can keep each individual fee earner up to date and provide incredibly quick accurate research their function has truly been superceded by technology. Maybe even partners will start doing their own research again if it is made quick and easy enough.

4. Admit that a lawyer doesn't need to be in the office to be working. PCs, laptops and the ability to connect to the Internet anywhere in the world make it easy to work anywhere. Up to now this has meant that a journey that was previously set aside for rest and relaxation is now scheduled work time. The other side of this coin is that there is no reason why on days with no meetings that a fee earner should not work from home. This would save the fee earner hours in commuting time and if the flexible working arrangements were the fee earners preferred option they could be an important reason to stay put when tempted by the huge offers of less flexible firms.

Taking things a step further a firm could employ an application service provider (ASP) to run some of the basic functions of the firm. An ASP runs a client's application on the ASP's own hardware, managed by the ASP's staff. All the firm needs are its PCs and web browsers. A firm can have all its accounting, payroll and expenses functions carried out on a third parties system. This can allow the firm to concentrate on its core functions, have access to a much more sophisticated IT system than would be possible in-house and to save on large-scale capital investment.

A further advance would be to hold all files online. Every document, phone message and scribbled note is scanned in to the firm's system. Once all files are held solely online the world of the Internet really does open up. One way this could be taken advantage of would be by having all taxations being completed online. The file is placed in a virtual taxing room and taxed online, saving money and time.

If all files are held online then the location of secretarial staff becomes largely irrelevant. This will also mean that all lawyers will need to be able to handle their own files online this in itself reducing the need for secretarial support. The existence of the lawyer that can't type will, at last, go the way of the dinosaurs.

If the use of the Internet in managing a law firm is taken to its logical conclusion the end result will be a virtual firm. This would involve going further than using an ASP to provide essential services or locating support workers away from the main offices to save on accommodation costs. It would involve outsourcing all the functions that could be separated from the main fee earning business. The fee earners would be left sitting alone in their much smaller offices, all other functions having been outsourced to more efficient providers. The majority of contact would be online, some essential IT and secretarial support would remain on site the rest would be employed and answerable to others and involved with the firm only because of their employers contractual relationship.

The idea of essentially outsourcing all but the essential fee earning capacity of a lawyer has been seized upon by those promoting the idea of virtual solicitors' chambers. Solicitors' chambers where groups of independent firms and sole practitioners share premises and resources to achieve economies of scale have now moved from the world of bricks and mortar to the virtual world. The first virtual solicitors' chambers (**http://www.solicitorschambers.co.uk**) intends to free the solicitor from all the administration, employment and other management issues leaving them free to focus on fee earning. This would involve all files being held online and a central office where all support staff would be housed. The solicitor paying approximately 20 per cent of their fee income to these virtual chambers. Small firms and sole practitioners are under huge pressures caused by rising overheads and falling income. The idea of a virtual solicitors' chambers offers a life-line to the small practice. It enables them to take advantage of economies of scale, to keep up with the benefits of new technology and to be able to cut down substantially on the proportion of time taken up with management issues and not spent fee earning.

In the near future it will be as unacceptable to say that you know nothing about new technology as it is to profess ignorance in reading and writing. While it is not necessary to know how to write a program or fix a broken computer, it is essential to understand the capabilities of the new technologies and how they can help lawyers carry out their legal and management functions. When multi-disciplinary partnerships are eventually given the green light it should come as no surprise to those in the know that some of the first non-solicitor partners will be IT professionals, probably not what the Law Society had in mind when the idea was originally floated.

The issues involved are twofold. The enormous opportunities to those that seize the ball and run with it and the question of survival for those that don't. Or put another way the firms that invest in new technologies and are continually rethinking how they do business will prosper. The ostriches with their heads in the sand will go to the wall.

CHAPTER TWO

WHAT NEXT?

How will the Technology Develop?

"The Web is far from done." Tim Berners-Lee

In this concluding section I intend to wander from the brief a bit and consider not only the future development of the Internet but also look at other areas of information technology that may affect a legal practice.

New developments don't generally come out of thin air. Inventors don't often have Eureka moments in the bath. The majority of paths that information technology will take over the next few years already exist. It is more a question of gradual progression until new products are accepted as standard technologies. Some will make the grade, others won't because of cost, technical problems or lack of consumer demand.

If you want to know more about what the new developments are, there are a lot of sites on the Internet to keep you up to date. I have listed a few below:

http://gartner.com: The Gartner Group is a leading authority on information technology, a lot of information on site.

http://neilcameron.co.uk: Neil Cameron is a legal technology consultant, some free and some subscriber information on site.

http://www.lawsociety.org.uk: Check out the information technology section after following the links for members. Sound information and links.

http://www.cloudnine.co.uk: Legal Technology Insider, an authoritative subscriber only publication.

http://www.scl.org.uk: The Society for Computers and Law. A subscriber only site packed with information on law and technology.

Taking a very non-technical look at the front runners in the race:

Speed and Permanence of Access

One innovation that will come and will save a lot of impatient tapping of the fingers is doing away with the ridiculous process of booting up. Why when a computer can play a video online from a web site in Vanuatu does it take 10 minutes to get online?

In time this will lead to permanent access to the Internet. The development of this was initially held back by telephone monopolies and government regulation but with the relaxation of the regulatory environment and the break up of the old monopolies prices have started to tumble. This will bring in time the collapse of the old pricing structures. No more charging by minutes or hours online. Your computer, whether at work or at home, will be permanently online, it will recognise you as you approach the screen, shake itself out of its idling mode and flip automatically to your home page.

Personalisation

One aspect of Internet technology that will be a growth area over the next few years is the personalisation of the Internet. Early examples are the personalised portal from Findlaw (**http://findlaw.com**). This enables you to choose the links that you need for your own personal portal. In time I would imagine that having your own portal would be the norm, certainly for professionals using the web. Using drag and click technology to drag links from all over the Internet to your own portal; it could be very simple. Another example would be the interactivity that is starting to be offered from online e-zines. The Law Society Gazette (**http://www.gazette.co.uk**) can be customised to the reader's interests. These two examples are just the start of a movement to make the Internet more personal to the user.

Click stream software is a name that will become more familiar over time. It is already here but the uses to which the information it gathers can be put are only just becoming apparent. Click stream software analyses, among other things, what web pages you read, how long you spend looking at them and what pages you download or print off.

It is capable of gathering huge amounts of information about an individual including their interests, political affiliations and idio-syncrasies.

Web pages will in time be able to respond to the person looking at them. If the web page uses data gathered from click stream technology it will know a lot about the person viewing the site even if they haven't visited the site before. Do they speak English? If not, the site will be automatically translated into their language. Maybe their interests are securities law, the opera and football. Using click stream software their online newspaper always headlines with their areas of interest. Or closer to home a firm has a practice web site, it receives a lot of through traffic but not much direct business is generated. Maybe if more was known about the visitors to the site then the site could be responsive to their interests whether they were environ-mental law, medical negligence or commercial conveyancing.

Push technology takes information gathered and uses it to work out what you are interested in with the purpose of then pushing to you other information in the same area. Push technology is not new in itself. It was initially used to send focused advertising, annoying everybody and eventually falling out of favour. But push technology doesn't have to be used to send advertising; the principle works equally well for ferreting out and sending specialist legal materials. So instead of you taking the initiative and adapting your portal or your e-zine, push technology could be used to automatically push new legal material in your specialist area to you.

Push technology and click stream software are both elements involved in making the Internet experience a more individual one. They and other technologies will be part of the drive towards making the Internet appear more manageable and personal to the user while at the same time providing opportunities to firms and lawyers to get more out of their Internet experience.

Connections

All the talk is of wireless, why be constrained by wires when the new broadband and ultrawide band technologies are opening up the Internet to those on the move? The boom in the market place is in mobile phones. It seems that every teenager in the country is busy sending text messages to each other on their mobiles. By 2003 there will be more than one billion mobile phones worldwide. With the new generation Internet access WAP (Wireless Applications Protocol) phones becoming commonplace it is only a matter of time before a lot of Internet access is wireless. First the WAP mobile phones, next the WAP personal digital assistants like the psion organiser and palm pilot and finally WAP laptops.

If more and more business is Internet or Intranet based and fee earners productivity increases with their mobility then the next logical step is the development of wireless laptops to enable a fee earner to be as productive on the move as they are at their desk.

The type of wireless technology that will support this development is on its way. The ultrawide band wireless technology is as quick as a wired Internet connection. It can give short range, high speed, wireless access to the Web over the air as fast as a wired connection. Wireless technology can allow a fee earner to access the Internet or the firms Intranet from a meeting anywhere in the building, no more fiddling with wires and connection points. With current technology and infrastructure this true mobility is limited to a geographic area of about three miles. But it is surely only a matter of time before truly mobile Internet access with unlimited access to data and unlimited roaming arrives.

When working at home or at your desk at work, wireless access is unnecessary. What is needed is the quickest land based access possible. There is a new option just coming on the market that is suitable for home and small business use. It will greatly increase the speed of Internet access enabling fast connection and downloading times even for complex multi-media applications. This is the Asymmetrical Digital Subscriber Line, or more simply, ADSL. This new technology is capable of transforming an ordinary copper phone line into a high speed digital line for ultra fast Internet access and as it uses your ordinary phone line you won't have to wait for all your roads to be dug up while cable is installed.

Searching

With the huge growth in the Internet, it is in danger of becoming unsearchable. It is just too big. This problem has led to a growth in the development of search engines. One of the solutions has been to create subject specific search engines like Lawrunner (**http://www. lawrunner.com**) and Lawcrawler (**http://findlaw.co.uk**). Both of these also limit their searches to named jurisdictions thereby further cutting down on the searchable material; making the process much more manageable. But given the explosive growth in the Internet, the sophistication of this type of search engine is just the start. The process of development will have to be continual to keep up with the pace of growth. The next phase needs to be the creation of intelligent search engines and browsers that don't only find the existence of a word in a document but can also assess the worth of this document.

A form of more directed searching that is entering the market is the e-bots or electronic robots. E-bots are intelligent robotic software agents that cruise the Internet. An e-bot automatically explores a targeted web site to look for new information. When new information is found it will automatically notify subscribers what is available. E-bots can be used to save the time and energy of lawyers. This can be done by automating the searching for important information and the disseminating of any information found to all necessary parties.

E-bots can be used in lots of ways. Examples would include using them to keep up to date. Say an e-bot was targeted on the Lord Chancellor's civil practice rules pages, then every time any change was made, notification would be given of the change and what that change was. Or an E-bot could be used to target the pages of a client to keep the firm up to date on any changes or even the web pages of a potential client.

The uses for E-bots are extensive and as part of a complete package of knowledge management systems in a firm they could prove very useful.

Voice Recognition

Voice recognition technology has never really worked. It has been waiting in the wings of main stream technology for a long time. It would appear that its time is eventually coming. On a computer near you soon it should be possible to speak and have your words translated accurately into writing. The true arrival of voice recognition technology will cut down even further on secretarial support in a firm. If a fee earner can speak into their computer and see their words translated onto the screen in front of them then the secretary's job will be reduced to tidying up and ensuring the letter is put in an envelope. With e-mails even this function disappears.

Another aspect of voice recognition technology that will have an effect on law firms will be the integration of messaging systems. No difference will be made between voicemail and e-mail. They will be seen as interchangeable media and the message will be accessible in whichever format is the most convenient.

Video Conferencing

The true availability, of video conferencing as an alternative to flying half way across the world for a meeting, depends on the technology available to support it. Once the technology is established it will hopefully become as easy as turning on a monitor.

C-Commerce

C-Commerce stands for collaborative commerce: a new form of e-business. It highlights a new way of thinking as much as any specific product. The idea behind collaborative commerce is to enable multiple enterprises to work together interactively online. It involves thinking afresh about relationships between competing firms. C-Commerce promotes, not surprisingly, collaboration and partnerships, agreements and joint ventures. In law firm terms it could involve the pooling of resources of several firms to create a truly impressive online provider of legal services, while at the same time maintaining separate bricks and mortar practices. Or maybe bringing together the skills of two competing but complimentary firms to offer a unique service online. The most important thing is that it involves a restructuring of relationships between competitors allowing them to work together when that is beneficial to all parties.

These are not all or maybe not even some of the most important developments that are going to happen in information technology over the next couple of years but they are a sample of some of the areas where a lot is happening at the moment. And as a consequence of this they might be worth watching to see what new ideas that might be of real benefit to lawyers and their practices emerge.

INTERNET SERVICE PROVIDERS

Below is a list of some of the most popular Internet Service Providers in the U.K. There are many other companies offering competitive rates and special offers which are worth looking out for.

BT Internet

URL: **http://www.btinternet.com**

E-mail: **support@btinternet.com**

Telephone: 0800 800001

Compuserve

URL: **http://7www.compuserve.com**

Telephone: 1 800 292 3900

Demon Internet

URL: **http://www.demon.net**

E-mail: **sales@demon.net**

Telephone: 020 83711234

U-Net Limited

URL: **http://www.u-net.net**

E-mail: **hi@u-net.com**

Telephone: 01925 484444

America On Line

URL: **http://www.aol.com**

Telephone: 0800 376 5432

Freeserve

URL: **http://www.freeserve.com**

Or pick up software disc from Dixons

Virgin

URL: **http://www.virgin.net**

Telephone: 0500 558 800

WHSmith Online

URL: **http://www.whsmith.co.uk**

Or pick up software disc from WHSmith.

GLOSSARY

The majority of Internet terminology does not set out to confuse but in many instances it was developed by computer boffins with little thought for the public using it. A lot of the terminology is based on acronyms that can be a complete mystery to the uninitiated. Life is easier if you are familiar with the following terms, then you can nod knowledgeably when someone else who doesn't really understand what they mean throws them into the conversation.

ADSL

An Asymmetric Digital Subscriber Line is an ordinary copper phone line that has been transformed into a high speed digital line for fast Internet access.

Adobe Acrobat Reader Software

A lot of forms and documents on the Internet are stored in Portable Document Format (pdf). In order to read these documents it is necessary to have software on your computer that can translate these documents into a readable form. Acrobat Reader Software is the most common type of this software. It can be downloaded free from **http://www.adobe.com**.

Bandwidth

The amount of information that a network can carry.

Bits

Stands for "Because It's Time". A reference to the need to exchange information quickly. Used as the measure of the speed of data transfer.

Bookmark or Favourites

A method for storing your favourite Internet sites on your computer called "Favourites" on Internet Explorer.

Boolean Connectors or Operators

Are codes used to assist search engines to find relevant material. The most common connectors are the words "and", "or" and "not". For instance, if a search was for injuries caused by dogs if the search engine supported Boolean connectors you would search for "dog" and "injury". This would throw up only documents where the two words both appeared.

Browser

A computer program you use to browse the World Wide Web.

BPS

Bits per second transmitted by your modem.

Bytes and Megabytes

A byte is the basic measurement for how a computer stores things. A byte is made up of eight bits.

Convergence

Internet, telephone and television technologies are coming together and soon you will be able to access all with a single device.

Cookie

A small file stored on your computer by an Internet site you have visited. Then when you return to the site another day your information is already available.

Domain

A domain is where a computer is. It identifies a particular part of the Internet.

Download

To transfer information from the Internet to your computer.

E-mail

Mail sent electronically across the Internet.

Extranet

An Extranet is a connection to a company's Intranet accessible to a specified user. The access to the Intranet can be open or limited.

FAQs

Frequently Asked Questions.

Firewall

A firewall is a security system comprised of a set of computer programs located at a gateway to a network. Its aim is to protect a private network from users from other networks.

Homepage

The page chosen by the user to be their default page.

Host

The computer your Internet Service Provider uses to connect you to the Internet.

HotDocs

Some forms on the Internet are stored in Hotdocs format. In order to be able to read these forms it is necessary to download software to translate the forms into a language your computer can understand. The software can be downloaded free from **http://www.hotdocs. co.uk**.

HTML

Hypertext mark up language—a coded language used to create web pages.

HTTP

Hypertext Transfer Protocol an agreed set of rules to improve the way the Internet works.

Hyperlinks or Links

Highlighted text or graphics on a web page that enable you at the click of your mouse to jump to another page within the same site or to a new web page.

Internet Explorer

One of the most popular Internet browsers from Microsoft.

Internet Service Provider

A company whose role is to sell access to the Internet.

IP

Internet Protocol—an internationally agreed set of computer instructions that ensures compatibility between computers on the Internet.

Intranet

A network of computers within a business that uses Internet technology and looks like the Internet.

Java

A programming language that allows small programmes to be sent over a network and will run on any machine.

MP3

This is a way of compressing sound that allows music to be downloaded easily from the Internet.

Netiquette

Basic standards of behaviour expected from Internet users.

Newsgroups

A discussion group on the Internet.

Portable Document Format (pdf)

Portable document format is a format that alot of documents on the Internet are stored in (see Adobe Acrobat Reader Software above).

Portal

A web site usually on a specific topic that acts as a gateway to linked topics.

POP

Point of Presence—the point where you can access the Internet from a particular service provider.

POP3

Post Office Protocol number 3—a method of sending e-mail.

PPP

Point to Point Protocol—method by which two computers talk to each other.

RAM

Random Access Memory. The memory your computer needs to carry out functions.

SMS

Short Messaging System is a way of sending short typed messages over a mobile phone. It is cheaper than making a call and therefore is used by every teenager in the land.

SnailMail

The type that involves envelopes and stamps.

Spamming

Sending unwanted information to thousands of computers at the same time.

Upload

To transfer information from your computer to another on the Internet.

URL

Uniform Resource Locator or an address on the Internet.

WAP

Wireless Application Protocol, a new system that enables mobile telephones to connect to the Internet.

Xml

eXtensible mark up language—a coded language used to create more interactive and adaptable web pages.

Zip

The most popular method of compressing files so they can be sent over the Internet. The only problem being when they arrive in your mailbox they will need unzipping. This is easy if you have the right software. You either need to download the latest version from **http:// winzip.com** or **http://zipmagic.com** or to buy WinZip, ZipMagic or similar software which makes it simplicity itself to unzip the files.

INDEX

215

Index

Index

Index

Index

Index

Index

Index

Index

Index

Index

Index

Index